I0605419

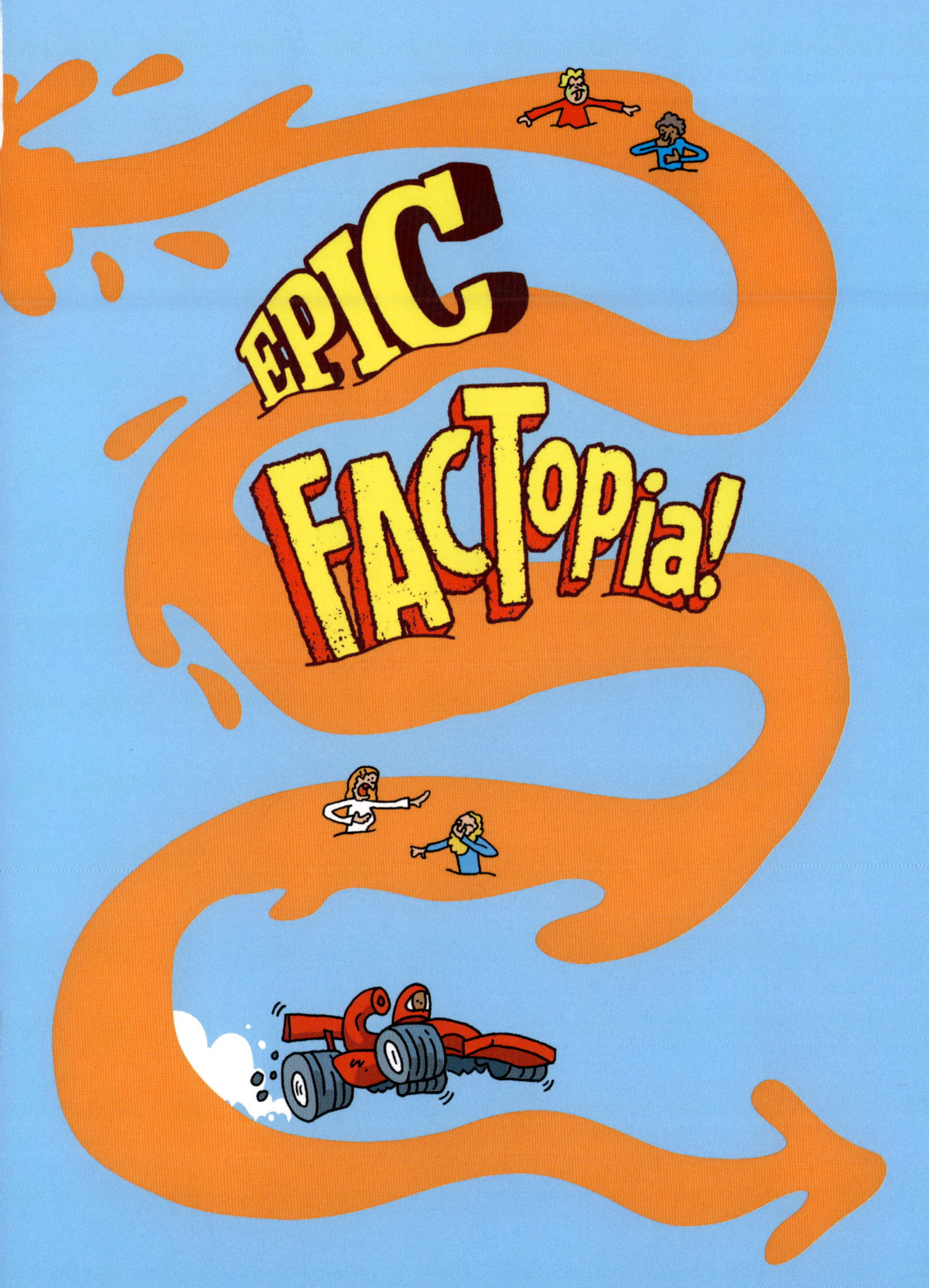
EPIC
FACTopia!

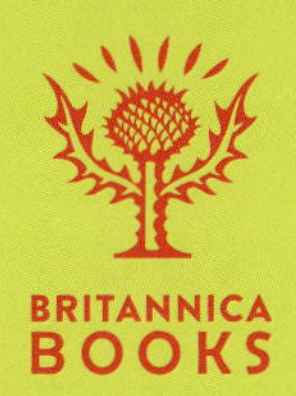

EPIC FACTopia!

Follow the TRAIL of 400 EXTREME FACTS

BY ROSE DAVIDSON

Illustrated by ANDY SMITH

CONTENTS

Welcome back to FACTopia!

Take your adventure to the limit as you journey through hundreds of mind-blowing, wow-worthy, and crazily cool facts about the universe's extremes. For example...

Did you know that the world's smallest frog could fit inside a human's belly button?

Small but mighty! The world's most painful sting comes from a 1-inch (2.5cm) critter called the bullet ant.

Ouch! In Costa Rica, a meteorite struck a doghouse, just missing the snoozing pooch inside.

Speaking of amazing survivors, divers rescued a ship's cook who had survived for three days by breathing from an air bubble that had formed inside his boat after it sank.

Rise up from the seabed! A Portuguese surfer once rode a wave that was taller than a ten-story building—the tallest wave ever surfed.

You might have spotted that there is something special about being here in FACTopia! Every fact is linked to the next, and in the most surprising and hilarious ways.

On this tour of incredible extremes, you will encounter deadly creatures, wacky laws, mega-rich pets, jaw-dropping records, and... well, you'll see. Discover what each turn of the page will bring!

But there isn't just one trail through this book. Your path branches every now and then, and you can go to a totally different (but still connected) part of the book by flipping backward or zooming forward.

Let your curiosity take you wherever you'd like to go. Of course, a good place to start could be right here, at the beginning

For example, take this detour to find out about superspeedy things

Go to page 48

The Challenger Deep, located in the Mariana Trench, is the deepest point in the ocean—it is deeper than Mount Everest is tall

Going deeper

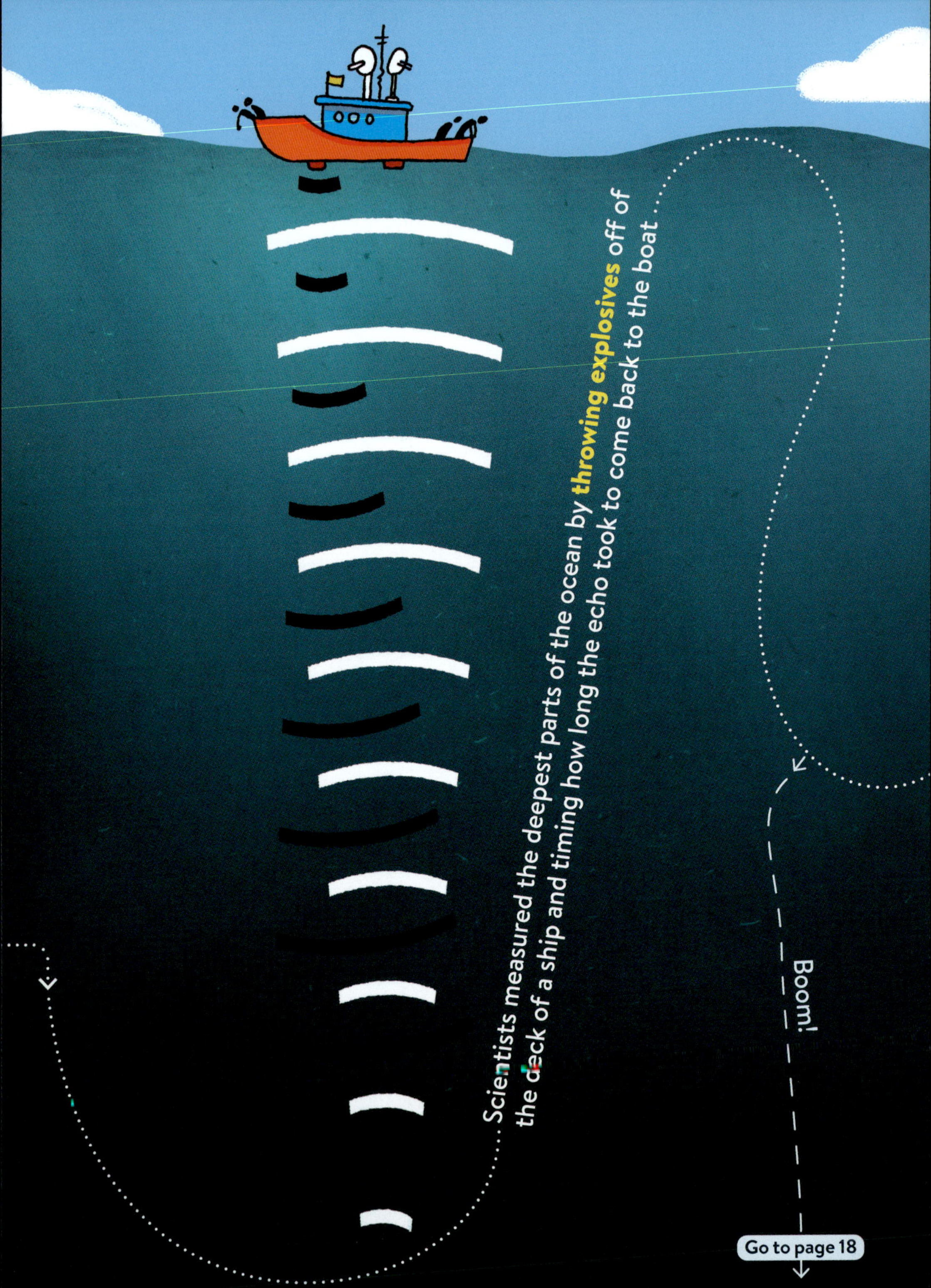

Scientists measured the deepest parts of the ocean by **throwing explosives** off of the deck of a ship and timing how long the echo took to come back to the boat

Boom!

Go to page 18

Climb up

Mountains in the ocean are called seamounts, and some humpback whales use them as landmarks to help navigate during their **long migrations**.

Named after the Norse god of thunder, Canada's Mount Thor is the steepest and tallest cliff on Earth, with a vertical drop of more than 410 stories
Check the forecast
Some extreme campers pitch their tents along cliff faces so that they hang off the sides of mountains as they snooze

A lightning bolt travels almost **1,200 times faster** than a Formula-1 race car zooms around a track

Swirling in the Indian Ocean for more than a full month and traveling some 5,000 miles (8,000km), Freddy was the longest-lasting **tropical cyclone** of all time

Storm chasers track **hundreds of tornadoes** a year as they whirl through Tornado Alley, an area in the middle of the U.S.A. that has the most tornadoes of anywhere in the world

The world's **biggest blizzard** lasted nearly a week and dropped up to 26 feet (8m) of snow in some areas of Iran—enough to snap power lines and crush vehicles.

Let it snow

One Victorian-era inventor created a device to predict when a storm was coming. It contained leeches that would hit a small hammer that would **ring a bell** when rain was approaching—and it worked.

Go to page 66

More planets

There are **SNOWSTORMS** on Mars.

At the Breckenridge International Snow Sculpture Championships, each competing team gets one 40,000-pound (18,144kg) **block of snow** to carve into a sculpture using hand tools like vegetable peelers, chicken wire, and saws

The professional sport of snowball fighting is called yukigassen, which means "snow battle" in Japanese.
Frost quakes—which can occur when temperatures drop rapidly and water in the ground freezes, causing the ground to expand—sound like
explosions
Ka-pow!

In 1815,
a mega-colossal explosion
erupted from Mount Tambora in Indonesia, and so much ash covered the planet that Earth didn't see summertime the following year.

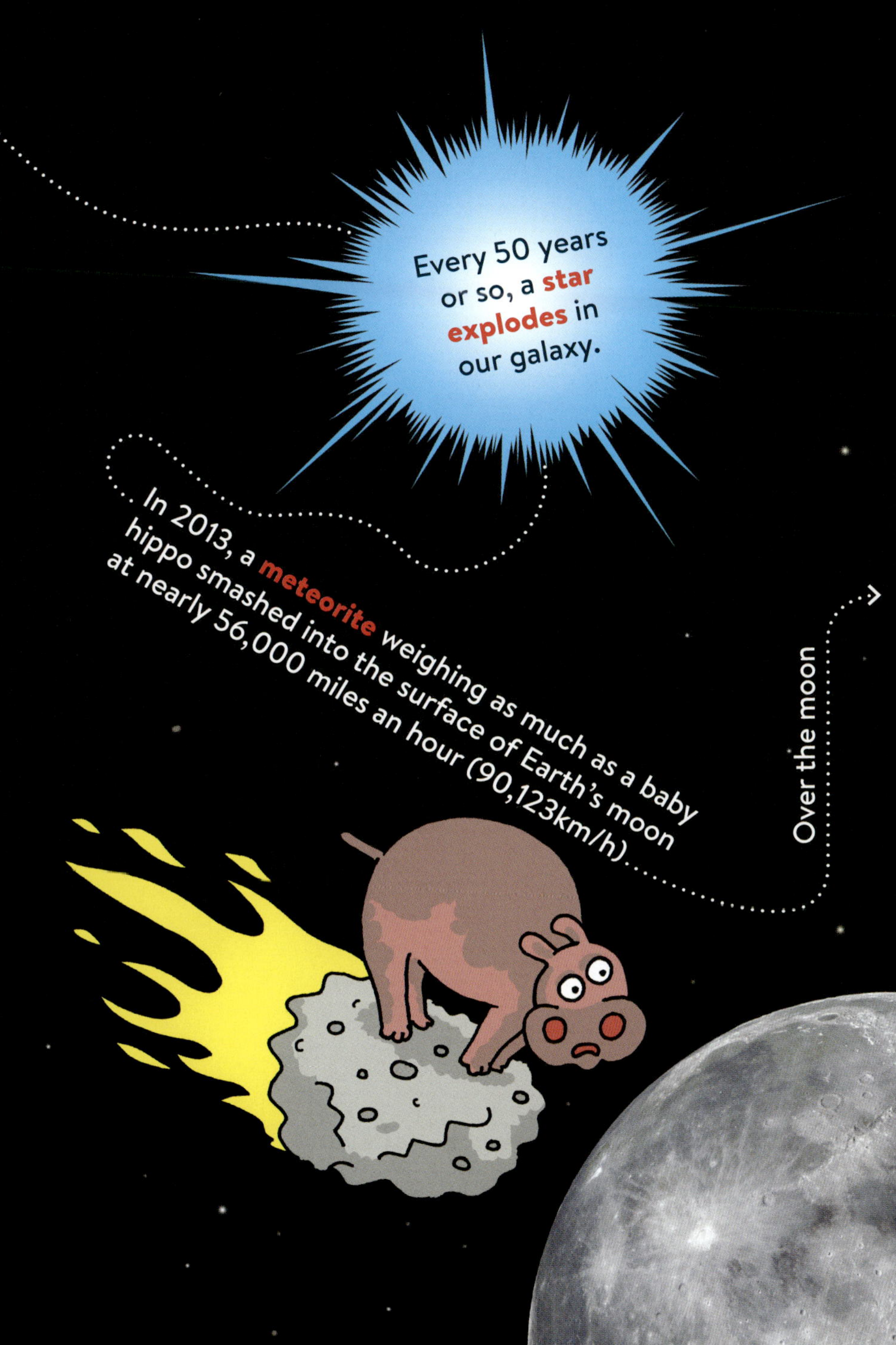
Every 50 years or so, a **star explodes** in our galaxy.
In 2013, a **meteorite** weighing as much as a baby hippo smashed into the surface of Earth's moon at nearly 56,000 miles an hour (90,123km/h).
Over the moon

Jupiter's moon Io—which has the most **volcanic activity** of any moon—looks like a pizza covered in melted cheese and olives

More eruptions
Go to page 60

Chile's Moon Valley has a **desert landscape** similar to the one on Earth's moon, so scientists test rover prototypes there

It's deserted

Earth's moon has enough water, found mostly in the **form of ice**, to fill at least 240,000 Olympic-size swimming pools

Male sandgrouses, a type of desert bird, fly up to 50 miles (80km) to collect water for their mate and chicks by **soaking it up** in their feathers

Desert-dwelling dorcas gazelles, which can live their entire lives without drinking water, have **solid pee**

A nonstop 135-mile (217km) race takes runners through **Death Valley**, a desert in California known for its record-high temperatures

A saguaro cactus—which is **covered with spikes** that reduce airflow and water evaporation to protect itself from extreme heat and cold—can grow taller than a five-story building

Go to page 32

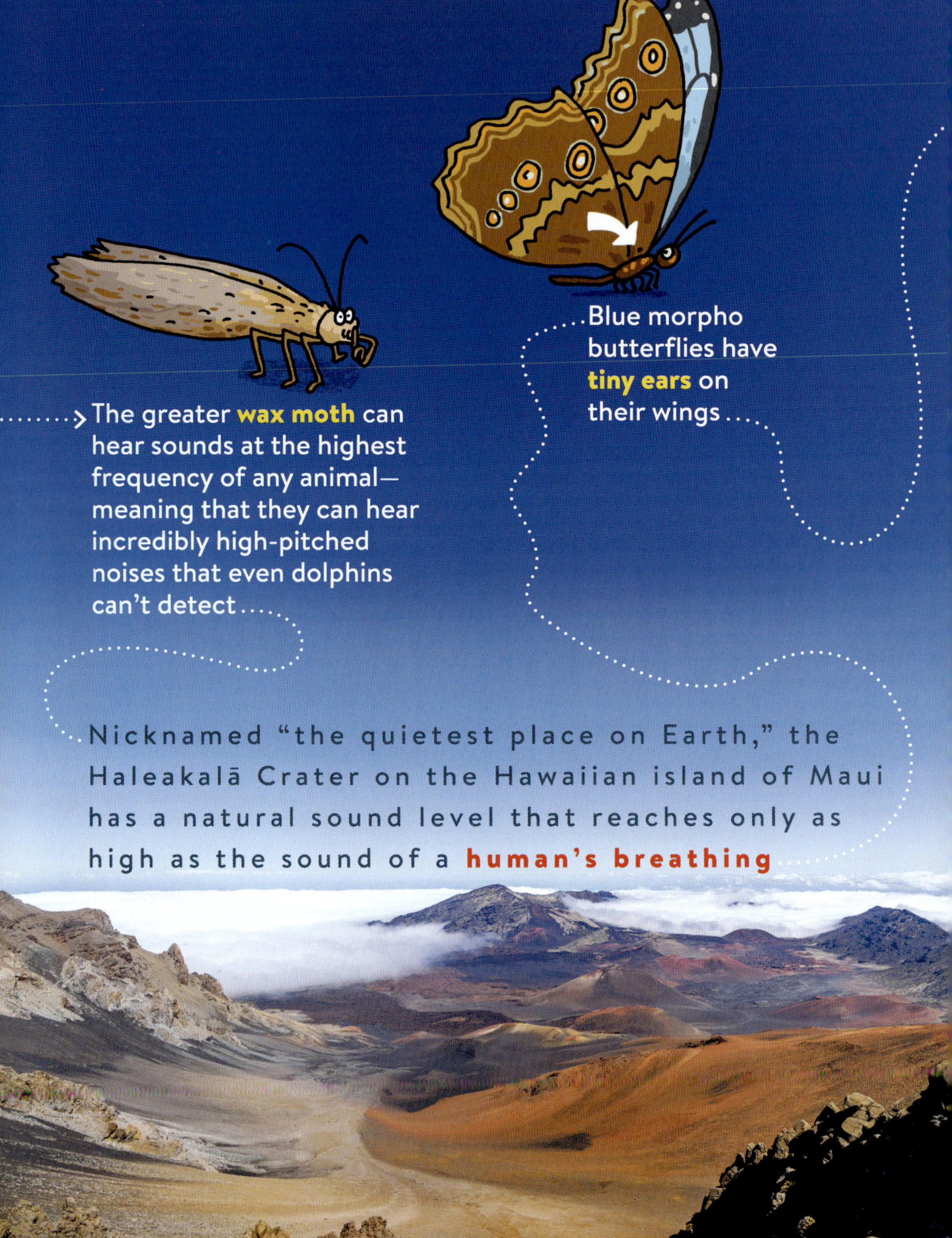

Blue morpho butterflies have **tiny ears** on their wings

The greater **wax moth** can hear sounds at the highest frequency of any animal—meaning that they can hear incredibly high-pitched noises that even dolphins can't detect

Nicknamed "the quietest place on Earth," the Haleakalā Crater on the Hawaiian island of Maui has a natural sound level that reaches only as high as the sound of a **human's breathing**

The world's loudest room is used to test how well **space hardware** can withstand the intense noise produced during rocket launches
Tweet! Tweet!
Male kakapos, birds found only in New Zealand, build **bowl-shaped holes** in the ground to help amplify their mating calls. They squawk loudly every night from these holes for three months straight

Huge swirling **storms** on Neptune produce 1,600-mile-an-hour **winds** (2,575km/h) and are so large they could swallow Earth whole.

Gigantic kites steered by computers are being used to harness **wind** energy to power **homes** with electricity.

Some birds can hear infrasound, or rumbles too low for humans to hear, which allows them to detect **storms** days before they happen.

Radar guided by **artificial intelligence** in the Arctic can detect and warn humans of approaching polar bears.

People who study **artificial intelligence** are looking to **snails**—which make choices using only two of the cells in their brain—to design more efficient robots.

An architect in Australia has designed a concept for eco-friendly homes called "poop houses" that collect and pump out human waste to automatically build the roof and walls.

Poop from an ocean animal called the bloody-belly comb jelly looks like glitter.

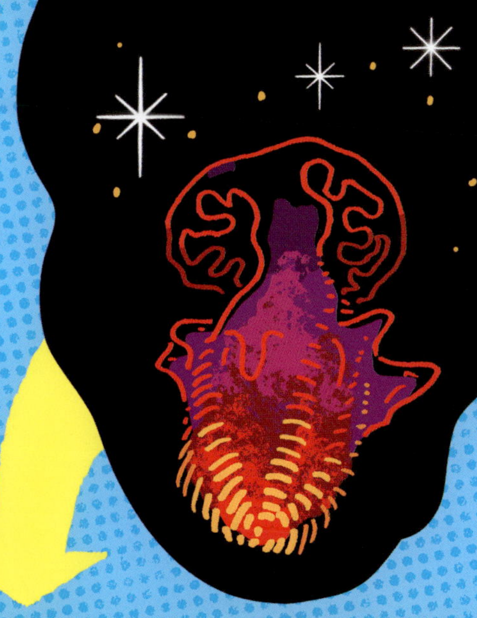

Chaff, tiny aluminum- or zinc-coated fibers that look like glitter, have been used by the U.S. military to scramble enemy radar.

Going micro

The world's smallest snail could fit through the eye of a needle.

The sharpest human-made object in the world is a needle that is only one atom thick at its point.

Go to page 58

Go slow

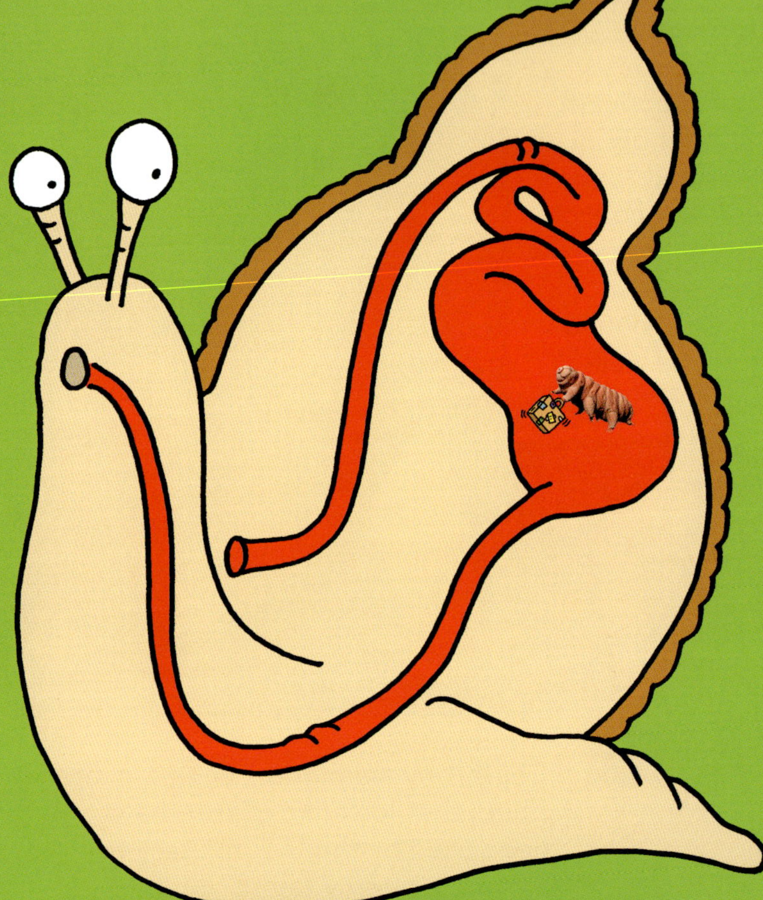

To move around, tardigrades will ride inside

SNAIL BELLIES,

and then get pooped out

In the waters of the Grand Prismatic Hot Spring at Yellowstone National Park, extreme-heat-loving microorganisms create beautiful

BANDS OF COLORS

Heating up

The Large Hadron Collider—a machine used by physicists to make particles **move faster**—can reach 7.2 trillion°F (4 trillion°C).

A supernova, an exploding star and the hottest natural thing in the universe, can be **6,000 times hotter** than the sun's core.

Lava flows in Hawaii can **bubble** at more than 1,600°F (870°C).

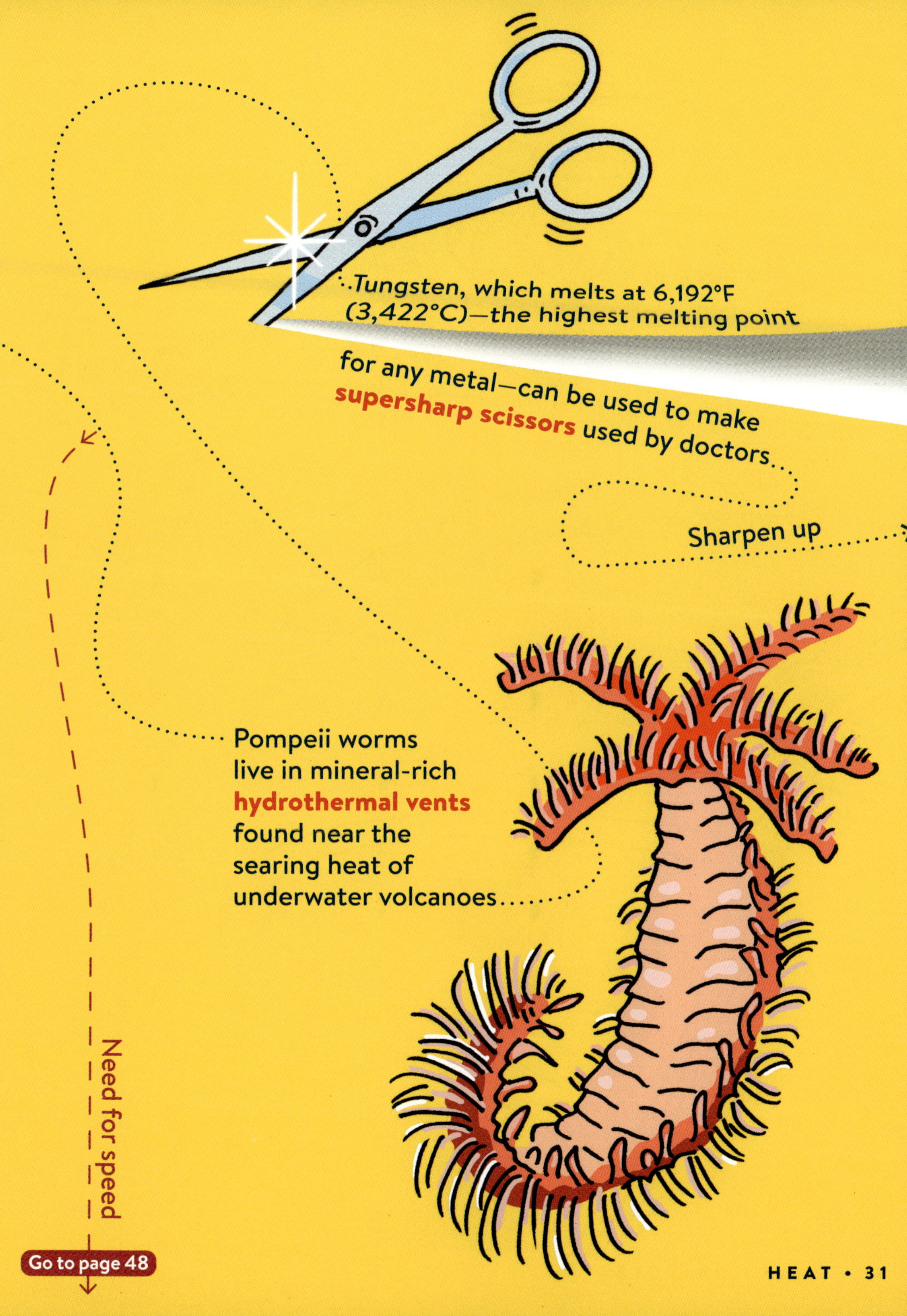

Tungsten, which melts at 6,192°F (3,422°C)—the highest melting point for any metal—can be used to make **supersharp scissors** used by doctors

Sharpen up

Pompeii worms live in mineral-rich **hydrothermal vents** found near the searing heat of underwater volcanoes

Need for speed
Go to page 48

Fossil records show that prehistoric **eellike creatures** had the sharpest-known teeth of any animal, with tips 20 times narrower than a single strand of human hair.

First used in the Middle East in the 11th century, steel Damascus swords were said to be sharp enough to slice a falling piece of silk in half and strong enough to **split stones**.

Cassowaries—considered the world's most dangerous birds—use their **sharp, daggerlike claws** to attack potential predators……

That rocks!

Go to page 54

Go to page 128

With the deadliest bite force of any animal, the saltwater crocodile can **chomp down** on a steak with more than 18 times the pressure of a human jaw...

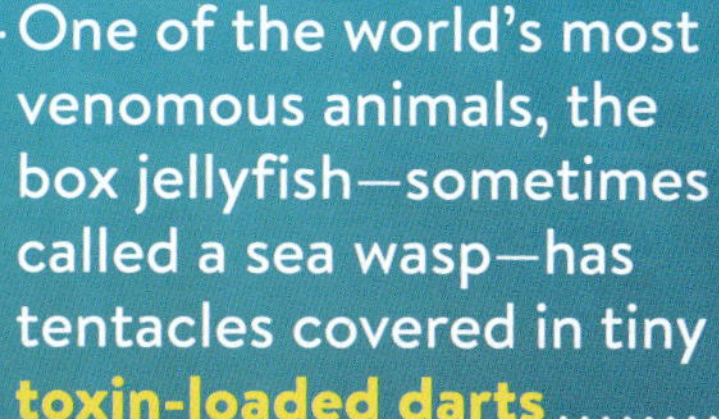

One of the world's most venomous animals, the box jellyfish—sometimes called a sea wasp—has tentacles covered in tiny **toxin-loaded darts** ...

Great white sharks—the ocean's deadliest predators—can smell a **single drop of blood** in 10 billion drops of water...

What's that smell?

Lesser anteaters, sometimes called
STINKERS OF THE FOREST,
are up to seven times smellier than skunks.
The hoatzin—also known as the
STINKBIRD
—reeks like cow manure.
Clouds on Uranus smell like
ROTTEN EGGS.

Mosquitoes are attracted to

SMELLY SOCKS

—the smellier the better.

Something's afoot

Chemists in Germany once produced a

SUPERSTINKY SUBSTANCE

that wafted through town and made people vomit, faint, and evacuate the area.

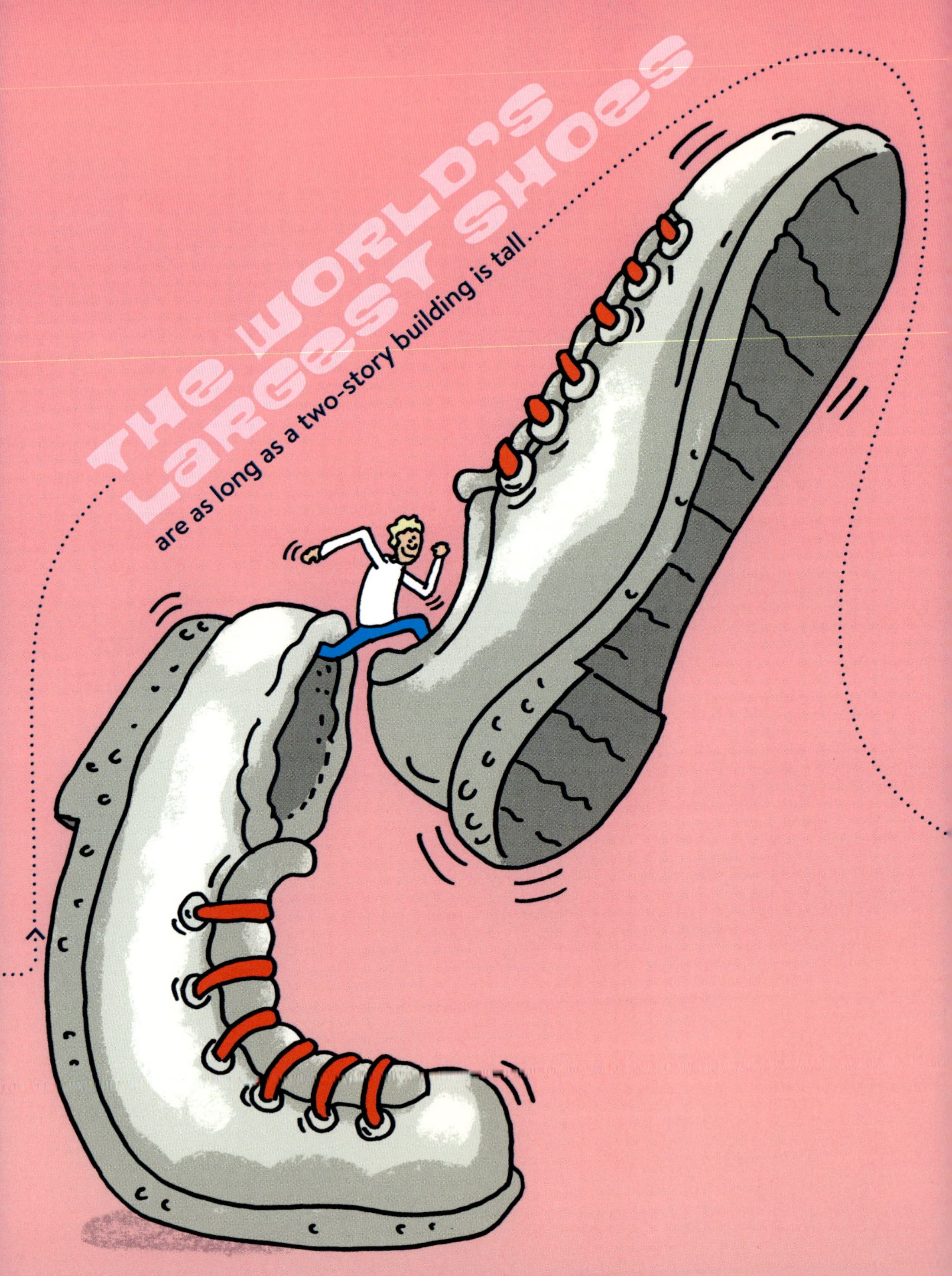
THE WORLD'S LARGEST SHOES
are as long as a two-story building is tall

An American man (and his dog) took seven years to walk around the world. He traveled nearly 30,000 miles (48,000km) and went through **45 pairs of sneakers**

A retailer in India once offered **high-heeled boots** that raised a person more than 1½ feet (50cm) off the ground

For 22 years, a man nicknamed the "**Planetwalker**" never used cars, buses, or other forms of motorized travel—instead, he walked everywhere he went . . .

. . . Canada's Great Trail, the world's **longest hiking trail** network, stretches more than 15,000 miles (24,000km)—sometimes using abandoned railways as its path . . .

Wooden wonders
Located in China, the "**plank walk in the sky**" is a dangerous hiking trail with narrow wooden pathways bolted to a steep mountainside. For safety, people hook themselves to chains that run along the trail's edge.

Not only do giraffes' long necks help them to reach food high in **trees**, but some scientists think their necks might also be so long because they're used like **swords** to battle each other.

The wood from purpleheart **trees**, found in the Amazon rainforest, is purple.

The **sword**-like tails of ancient sea **scorpions** were pointy and had toothed edges that might have been used to both spear and saw through prey.

Scientists want to build a **space** elevator that could carry **pods** of people along superstrong cables as they travel in and out of Earth's orbit.

When in bloom, some **orange** poppy flower fields can be seen from **space**.

A room at the world's first **pod** hotel in the **city** of Osaka, Japan, is just big enough for one person to sleep in.

Roughly 25 times brighter than the sun, Sirius A—also known as the **Dog** Star—is the brightest **star** in our galaxy.

In a **city** in Canada, energy created from **dog** poop is used to power some homes.

Australia is home to **species** that have some of the deadliest venom on the planet, including the blue-ringed octopus—its venom is 1,000 times more powerful than cyanide.

Biologists who study the bacteria in bat guts can identify some **species** just by the **color** of their poop.

The desert **scorpion**, found in **Australia**, makes a burrow about 3 feet (1m) deep and shaped like a spiral.

The oldest known **color** pigment is bright pink—researchers in West Africa found 1.1-billion-year-old fossilized bacteria with the pigment **inside**.

Thousands of bags of candy-coated chocolates rained down from **inside** a 47-foot-tall (14m) piñata shaped like a giant **orange** M&M, at a company event in New York City.

Star-nosed moles can smell underwater by blowing **bubbles** and then quickly inhaling them—a specialized strategy to detect odors from nearby prey.

La Bomba, a scorching-hot river in the Amazon rainforest, has **bubbling** water warmer than 200°F (93°C)—almost hot enough to boil.

Amazing Amazon

Go to page 178

Defend yourself!

The world's most painful insect sting comes from a 1-inch (2.5cm) critter called THE BULLET ANT...

A toucan's beak contains a **network of blood vessels** that helps cool down the bird like a built-in air conditioner in its humid rainforest home...

In the Amazon River, one of the largest rivers in the world, **giant water lilies** can grow as wide as a surfboard is long...

At birth, a pygmy marmoset—the world's smallest primate—is about as small as an adult human's thumb.
Getting smaller
Giant river otters prowl around the Amazon River, where they can catch and devour caimans.

Panda mothers typically weigh 900 times more than their newborns, while humans are only about 20 times heavier than their babies.

At less than one-third of an inch (7.7mm) long, the world's smallest frog can fit inside a **HUMAN BELLY BUTTON**

The heart of the Etruscan shrew, the world's smallest land mammal,

BEATS FASTER

than any other mammal's heart...

5546324487775 × 1245634891236=
6,908,595,300,089,175,536,639,900
The person who holds the Guinness World Record for the fastest
"HUMAN COMPUTATION"
could multiply two 13-digit numbers in under 30 seconds...
In 2006, the fastest rocket launch in history sent the New Horizons spacecraft hurtling toward the sky more than 150 times faster than a Formula-1 race car.
Nifty numbers

Go to page 74

The world's fastest window cleaner could squeegee roughly one window every three seconds...
Awesome work

Some ferrets have been trained to run wires and cables
through small places where humans can't fit

Speleologists, scientists who study caves, are exploring the hottest caves on Earth to get a better idea about what **life on Mars** might be like.

Down, down, down

A **scuba-diving pizza delivery** person delivers food inside an airtight case to an underwater hotel in Florida . . .

Specially trained to fight wildfires, smokejumpers **parachute from planes** to reach the site of a blaze . . .

Known for their **supersmarts**, capuchin monkeys have been trained to help people perform daily tasks, such as turning on an appliance or dialing a phone . . .

In 2018, an international team of cave divers **rescued a soccer team** from a flooded cave in Thailand

A blind, **cave-dwelling salamander** called an olm can live for more than 100 years

At 92 feet (28m) long, the longest

FREE-HANGING STALACTITE

formed inside a cave in Minas Gerais, Brazil

Rock on!

Northern Ireland's Giant's Causeway—a series of 40,000 interlocking columns of basalt rocks—is named for a **mythical giant** that supposedly hurled the rocks into the sea to build a path that would reach another giant in Scotland . . . . . .

More magnificent myths
Go to page 168

In Costa Rica, a meteorite once struck a doghouse, just missing the snoozing pooch inside
Take cover!

Some bunkers—shelters designed to protect people against potentially catastrophic events—have luxurious features such as pools, water parks, theaters, and gyms below the **ground**.

The person who achieved the world's lowest limbo was just 8½ inches (22cm) from the **ground**, about as high as a soccer **ball**.

The Kilimanjaro **water** slide in Brazil launches water-park **visitors** from 16 stories high at speeds of roughly 62 miles an hour (100km/h).

Over the course of several years, **visitors** to a bridge in France decorated it with roughly 700,000 padlocks—equaling the **weight** of about 20 elephants—to symbolize love.

With a **weight** of only 6½ pounds (3kg), one of the smallest dinosaurs—nicknamed "pretty jaw"—had a **body** only slightly larger than that of a modern chicken.

Wallace's giant bees (which are four times bigger than honeybees) scrape their massive jaws on trees to collect **balls** of resin and **wood** for their nests.

A woodpecker can drill its beak into **wood** more than 8,000 times in a single day as it looks for **food** to extract with its sticky tongue.

To spice up their **food**, ancient Aztec people made an early version of hot sauce with **water** and chili peppers.

Giant ground sloths—extinct ancestors of today's sloths—were so big that they could swallow **avocados** whole. Avocado plants still grow today because the sloths spread the seeds in their poop as they moved.

Slow down

Scientists discovered the skull of a prehistoric big-eyed lizard—whose **body** was likely smaller than an **avocado**—that had been preserved in amber for 99 million years.

Sea anemones rarely move—but when they do, they sometimes do very slow **somersaults** in the water

It would take 20 minutes for the world's **slowest tortoise**—a giant tortoise in Seychelles—to walk the length of a football field

About to blow

The Stromboli volcano, in Italy, has been slowly erupting for centuries, spewing out

SMALL BURSTS

of ash, fragments, and rocks from its three active craters.

Two athletes wore gas masks to avoid breathing in **toxic fumes** while they set a record for the longest slackline over an active volcano.

Mauna Loa, which means "long mountain" in Hawaiian, is the world's **larges**

active volcano, with an average of one eruption every five years

In the sport of **EXTREME IRONING,** people attempt to smooth clothing in challenging places, including in the sky or underwater ...

A person on a mission to make **competitive chair sitting** an official sport once sat in a desert for 14 hours and 27 minutes ...

Go to page 136

In Oymyakon, Russia, the coldest inhabited place on Earth,
SALIVA CAN
FREEZE
on a person's lips when they walk outside

Walruses, which live in the chilly waters of the Arctic, can **slow down their heartbeat** to survive in supercold temperatures.
Into space
Uranus is the **coldest planet** in our solar system, with temperatures dipping as low as -371°F (-224°C)

Discovered in 2015 around Halloween, an icy **dwarf planet** nicknamed "the Goblin" is about two and a half times farther from the sun than Pluto and one-tenth the size of Earth's moon . . . .

Valles Marineris on Mars is the **largest canyon system** in the solar system—it is nine times as long and three times as deep as Earth's Grand Canyon . . . .

Down low

Go to page 8

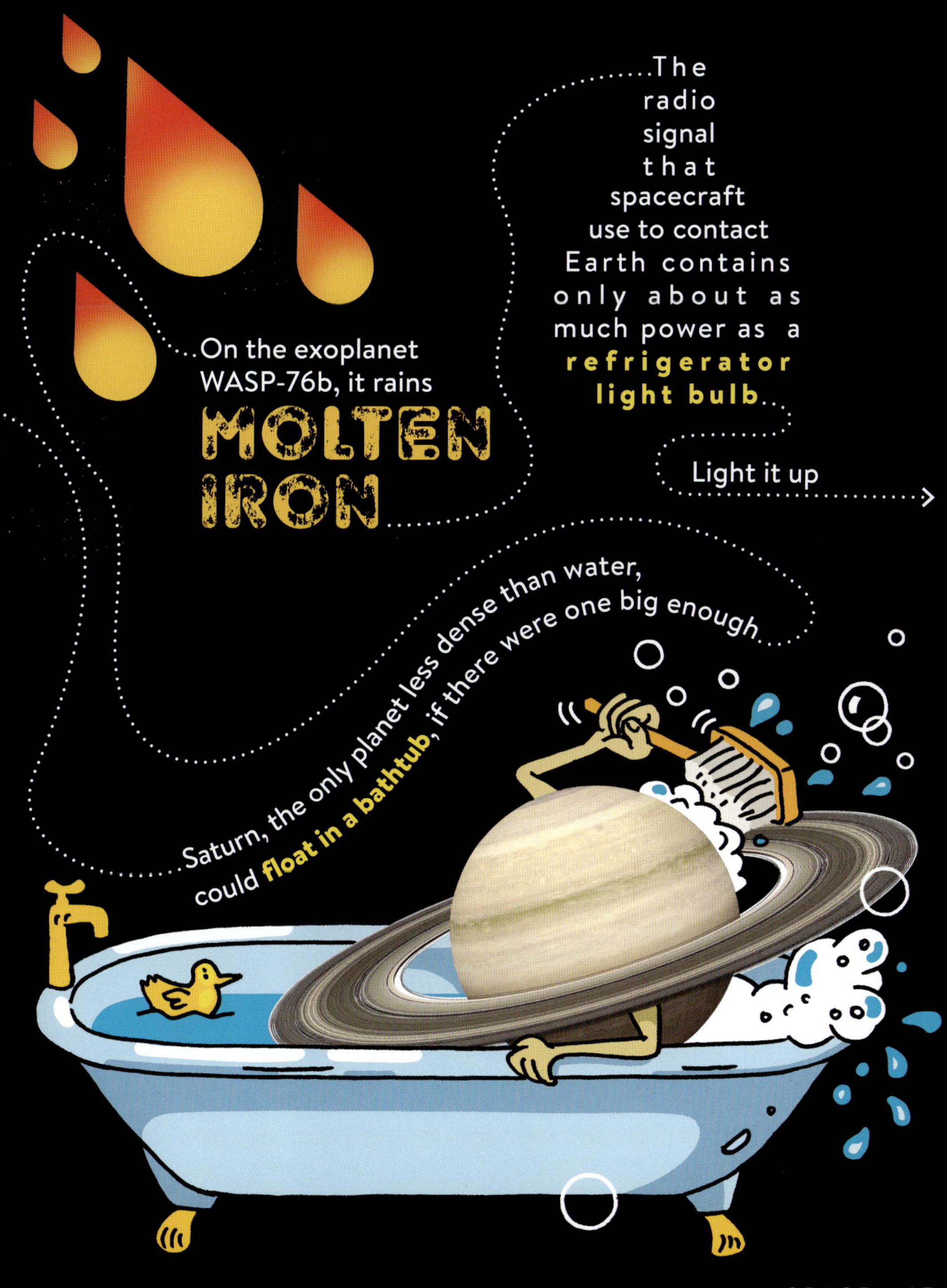
On the exoplanet WASP-76b, it rains
MOLTEN IRON
The radio signal that spacecraft use to contact Earth contains only about as much power as a refrigerator light bulb.
Light it up
Saturn, the only planet less dense than water, could float in a bathtub, if there were one big enough.

Using blue lights, scientists discovered that turtles can

glow in neon colors

Scientists in a lab created a light that's a billion times brighter than the surface of the sun

Going dark

Invented by scientists, Vantablack is one of the **darkest shades of black** on Earth—it absorbs 99 percent of the light that reaches it

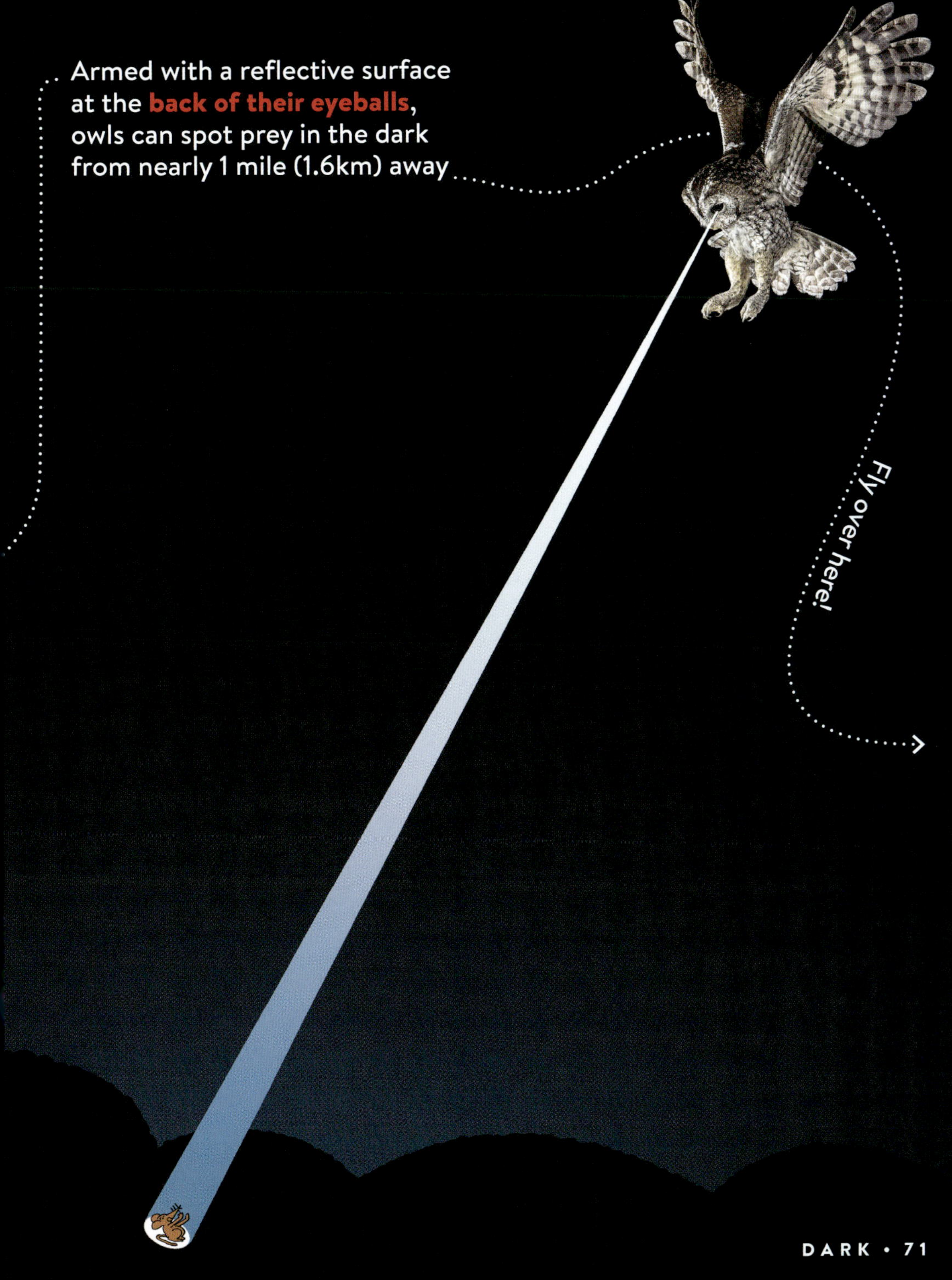
Armed with a reflective surface at the **back of their eyeballs**, owls can spot prey in the dark from nearly 1 mile (1.6km) away
Fly over here!

A pilot managed to fly an airplane through a tunnel at the

RECORD SPEED

of 152 miles an hour (245km/h)

A person riding a **hoverboard** in France once flew farther than 7,300 feet (2,225m).

Go figure!

024259506950647383956574791365193517983345353625214300354

A number known as "**Graham's Number**" has so many numerals in it that, if written

…2677162267216041981065226316…

…out, it wouldn't fit in the observable universe

Valued at $23 million, the toilet on the International Space Station is the **most expensive toilet in the universe**. Specialized foot restraints and handholds help keep astronauts in place while they use it.

So fancy!

Archaeologists discovered a 3,700-year-old gravesite in Spain containing a woman's skeleton draped in necklaces and bracelets and wearing a **crown**.

The **crown** of golden feathers, known as a crest, on the **head** of the gray-crowned crane splays out like a pom-pom.

The hammerheaded bat has a large moose-like **head** on top of its **body**.

An artist made a hat that reached a **height** of almost 16 feet (4.8m), an **accessory** that is taller than the average school bus.

The oldest-known purse, an **accessory** dating back 4,500 years and found in what is now Germany, was decorated with dog **teeth**.

Armed with bladelike **teeth**, saber-toothed **cats** could pierce through their prey with a single bite.

Ciorani, Romania, is known as the **cat** capital of the world because there are four cats for every one person in **town**.

Spotted breaking into homes in a California **town**, a 500-pound (227kg) black bear nicknamed "Hank the Tank" became famous for searching for leftover **pizza** and other treats.

Some sharks can sleep without closing their **eyes**, snoozing for short naps both day and **night**.

In the **night** sky, a rare phenomenon called a jellyfish sprite looks like a giant flashing marine **animal**.

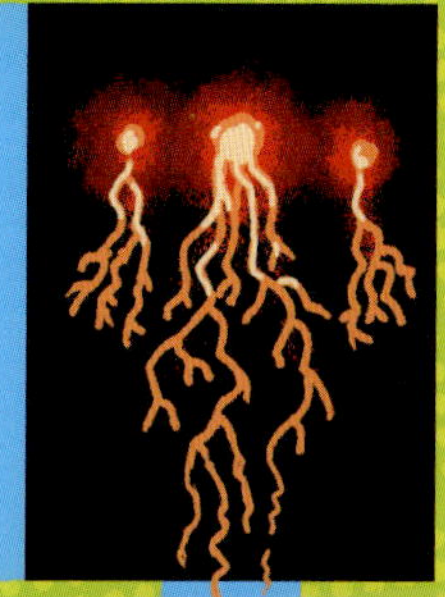

In the Great Barrier Reef, the world's largest coral reef system, marine **animals** called corals spawn together in massive numbers once a year after a full **moon**.

Jumping robots could one day explore the **moon**, where their springs would launch them more than 400 feet (122m) high in low gravity—four times the **height** they can reach on Earth.

Though a tarsier's **body** is small—roughly 4 inches (10cm) long—its **eyes** are huge. In fact, they are so big that they cannot move in their sockets, but instead a tarsier rotates its head 180 degrees in either direction to look around.

One Italian chef creates **pizza** portraits of celebrities using only dough, **tomato** sauce, and cheese.

Weighing more than 10 pounds (4.5kg), the world's biggest **tomato** was heavier than the average newborn baby.

Quokkas are sometimes called the **world's happiest animals** because they look like they're smiling when they pant

Cuteness aggression—a feeling of wanting to **squeeze something until it pops**—is an involuntary response in the brain that happens when we're overwhelmed by a positive feeling

Human babies are born with nearly **fully grown eyes**, so they appear bigger compared to other body parts. This triggers many humans to feel joy and an urge to protect and nurture

Growing up

After being born, **kangaroo joeys** live in their mom's pouch, where they eat, sleep, and poop for months without leaving.

DAY 1

DAY 14

The **turquoise killifish** goes from baby to fully grown in only 14 days

A rare plant called the

Queen of the Andes

can take up to 100 years to grow flowers

Beautiful blooms →

Russian scientists found seeds that had been buried 32,000 years ago by an

ICE AGE SQUIRREL

and used them to grow new plants

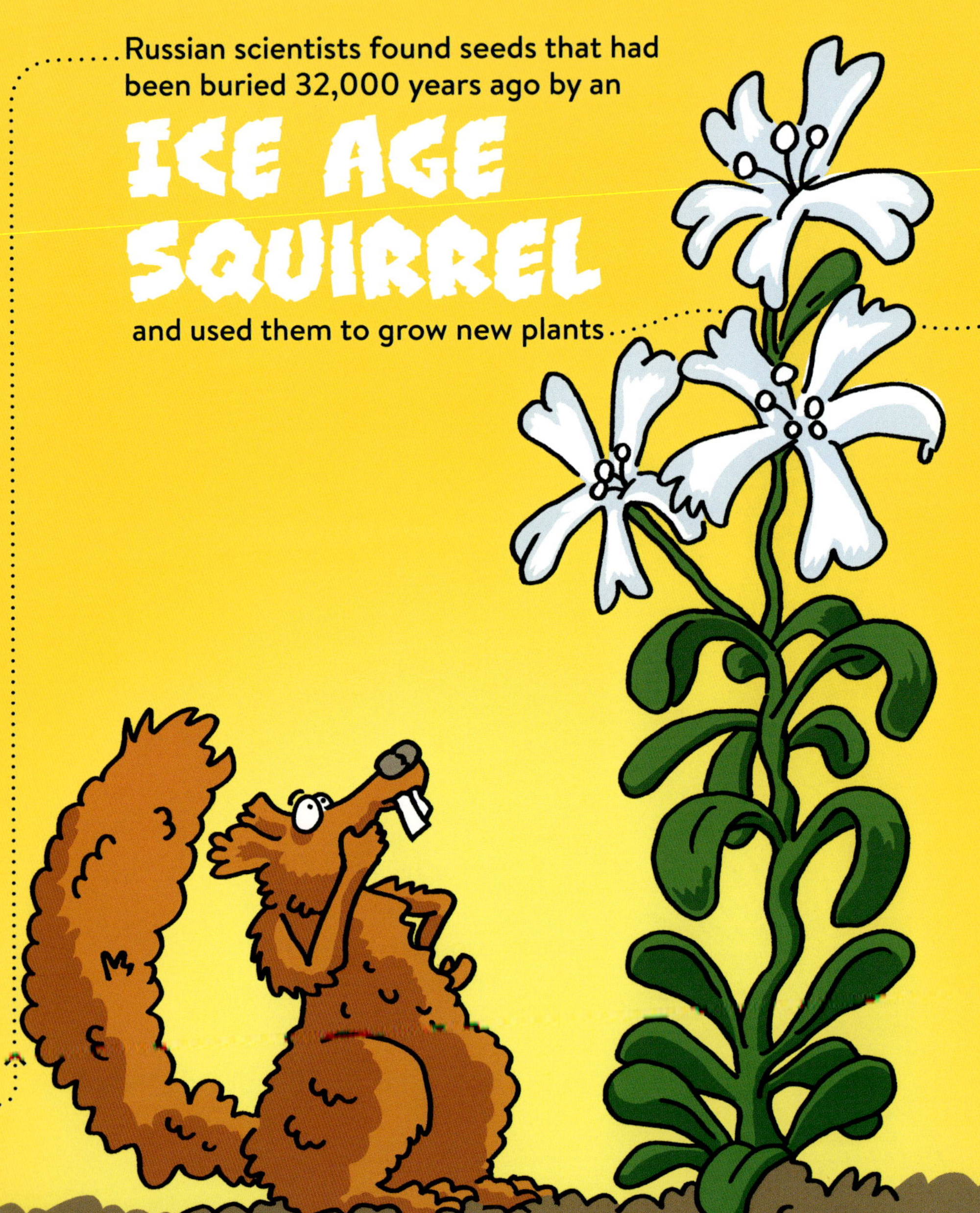

The world's smallest flowering plant, the watermeal, is about the size of a **grain of rice**.

When it rains after a drought in parts of Australia, **poached egg daisies**—named so because of their yolky yellow middles and white petals—are some of the first flowers to grow.

The gas plant has flowers that give off a **lemon-scented oil** that can be set on fire.

Marigolds were used by the Aztecs to cure the hiccups and to soothe people who had been **struck by lightning**.

Eggs-traordinary!

Extinct **elephant birds** laid some of the largest animal eggs ever known, reaching 13 inches (33cm) long and weighing up to 22 pounds (10kg).

Ostrich eggs
have the thickest
shell of any
birds—they are
as thick as two
pennies.
Some fish eggs can survive being eaten and pooped out by ducks
Against the odds

Some scientists think tardigrades are likely the only animals that would survive an
APOCALYPTIC EVENT
such as a meteor collision.....

Plant power

Some plants in New Zealand can survive in **volcanic soil** that heats up to 162°F (72°C)

After his boat sank 100 feet (30m) below the water's surface, a ship's cook survived for three days by **breathing from an air bubble** that formed inside the vessel, before he was rescued by divers

Go to page 192

Incredible insects

The cobra lily, which resembles the snake it's named for, is a carnivorous pitcher plant that **DEVOURS INSECTS**

At the World Nettle Eating Competition in the U.K., contestants battle to see who can pluck and eat as many **raw stinging nettle leaves** as possible, bugs included

Wildflowers called prairie smoke look like tiny **bits of cotton candy**.

Although its stalks are safe to eat, the rhubarb plant has leaves that are both sour and **extremely poisonous**.

More lip-smackers

The seeds of some tropical trees can be **carried by currents** from one side of an ocean to the other, where they can sprout.

Umeboshi,

pickled plumlike fruits

that come from the ume tree, are three times more sour than lemons...

The extremely

SOUR JUICE

of the bitter melon
is used to help fight
some illnesses

Sweeten things up

Terrific trees

Go to page 160

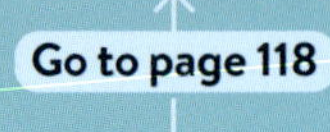
Go to page 118

How special

In Dubai, United Arab Emirates, you can buy an **$800 scoop of vanilla ice cream** mixed with expensive ingredients such as saffron and black truffle and sprinkled with gold-leaf flakes.

The top of the world's **tallest ice-cream cone**, built in Norway, reaches as high as a basketball hoop...

Confectioners constructed an 18,000-pound (8,165kg) **chocolate replica** of an ancient Maya temple in Mexico

The **largest-ever candy bar** weighed more than 5,900 pounds (2,676kg) and reached 9 feet (2.7m) long

Some bakers have created wedding cakes shaped like **majestic castles**—they often take about eight hours to build and some require five trucks to transport them

What a fort!

At an annual festival in China, thousands of workers have created towering castles entirely out of

ice blocks

Go to page 30

That's hot!

Inside the ancient Nakhal Fort in Oman, soldiers once waited in **hidden nooks** to pour cauldrons of searing-hot honey or date juice on approaching invaders

Visitors to a sandcastle hotel in the Netherlands can sleep in a room with **sand walls and floors**. There is even a drawbridge and turrets

Sandy shores

A massive 425-foot-long (130m) sculpture of a **sea serpent's skeleton**

curves through the water near the coast of Nantes, France.

So bony!

The **blue whale** may be the biggest animal on the planet, but it typically **swims** at a speed of only 5 miles an hour (8km/h).

The **blue whale's** jawbone, or mandible, is the biggest bone of any animal on Earth—one town in Scotland even turned one of these bones into an archway.

With a price as **high** as $1.7 million, the "Titan Zeus" **television** weighs just under a ton and measures nearly 31 feet (9m) from corner to corner.

While being filmed for a **television** talk show, a person once carved 109 **pumpkins** in just one hour—the most jack-o'-lanterns ever carved in that amount of time.

Contestants in the U.S.A. once shot **pumpkins** out of catapults and air cannons to see whose traveled the farthest during an international **competition**.

The backswimmer is an insect that gets its name because it **swims** upside down on its **back**.

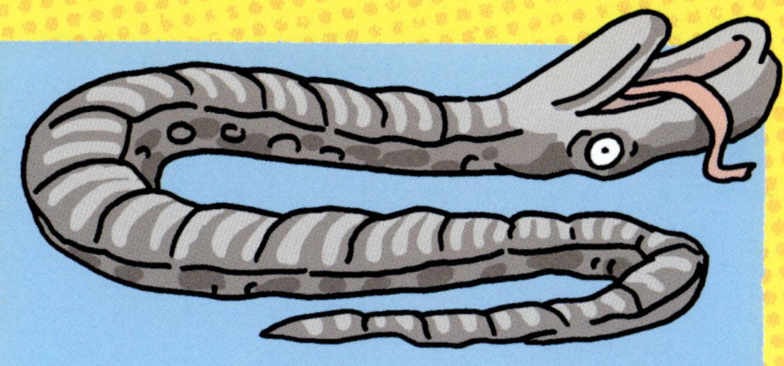

When threatened, an eastern hognose snake may flip over on to its **back**, open its mouth, and even emit a **foul smell** to trick a predator into thinking it's dead.

The **foul smell** that an **insect** called a shore earwig releases when bitten smells like rotting flesh and poop.

The largest swarms of **insects** are formed by desert locusts, which can gather in numbers as **high** as 70 billion.

Every year in Scotland, teams of golden retriever dogs and their owners enter a tug-of-war **competition** at the Golden Retriever Festival.

Feeling festive?

During the **fireworks show** at Japan's Katakai Festival, explosives that bloom up to 2,400 feet (732m) wide light up the sky

In India, the **world's longest festival**—Bastar Dussehra—lasts 75 days and celebrates the goddess Danteshwari

Each summer in Buñol, Spain, tens of thousands of people gather, armed with tomatoes, for La Tomatina—the **world's biggest food fight.**
Eat up!

The **Dragon's Breath chili** is one of the world's hottest peppers. It's roughly 1,000 times hotter than a jalapeño...

Cheese is the most shoplifted food in the world—reportedly around 4 percent of all cheese made ends up stolen...

A factory in Bahrain created the world's largest **OREO cookie**, which was more than 6,000 times bigger than a regular-size OREO...

Grown exclusively in Italy, a white **Alba truffle**, a type of edible fungus, can sell for up to $330,000...

Sweet!

Go to page 92

A former grocery-store worker has collected more than 30,000 stickers from pieces of fruit.
So collectable

A collector nicknamed "Hamburger Harry" owns more than 3,700 burger-related items, including a

hamburger-shaped motorcycle

Back in time

The world's largest collection of coprolites—also known as fossilized poop—includes a

puppy-size poop

from a prehistoric crocodile.

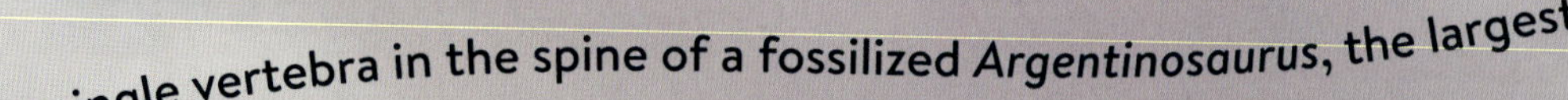

A single vertebra in the spine of a fossilized *Argentinosaurus*, the largest

Nicknamed for their birdlike appearance, "ostrich dinosaurs" were the fastest prehistoric creatures on land, able to run **as fast as modern lions do** ...

and animal ever found and the world's biggest dinosaur, is the size of an adult human.

Float your boat

The head of *Sarcosuchus*, a prehistoric **dino-eating crocodile**, was the inspiration behind the sleek design of a luxury yacht

A concept for a $1 billion mega yacht named *The Streets of Monaco*—modeled after the country of Monaco, in Europe—is a "**floating city**" with its own racetrack.

A musician in Sydney, Australia, commissioned a

GUITAR-SHAPED BOAT

Keep strumming

Static electricity can build up in people during dust storms. During America's 1930s Dust Bowl, there was sometimes so much static that people could knock each other out as they shook hands!

You can bend a stream of water using the static electricity that is built up when you rub an inflated balloon against your hair.

A massive dust plume that forms every year in Africa was so big in 2020 that it was nicknamed the "Godzilla dust cloud."

At the moon's equator, temperatures can reach above the boiling point of water on Earth!

Some creators of the famous giant lizard-like Godzilla originally thought of making him a monstrous octopus instead.

A mechanical pencil that was carried to the moon on the Apollo 15 space mission sold for $5,000.

Fifteen octopuses, of a species called the gloomy octopus, built an underwater "city" out of shells and sand, where they all lived together.

One man built a working electric guitar out of 2,000 colored pencils.

The city of Fort Bragg, California, is home to Glass Beach—where millions of pieces of colorful sea glass are mixed in with the sand.

At just under 2 feet (56.7cm) tall, Bombel, a miniature Appaloosa from Poland, is the world's shortest **horse**—he is shorter than a **greyhound** dog.

Greyhounds first arrived in the Americas on **boats**, with Christopher Columbus.

Xerxes I, an ancient Persian ruler, transported his army across a river by lining up 676 **boats** to form a huge bridge.

Crossing over

Once a year, in Massachusetts, antique vehicles, including **cars**, airplanes, and even stagecoaches pulled by **horses**, race against each other.

At the **Balloon** World Cup, players bat a balloon into the air without letting it hit the ground, avoiding obstacles like furniture, a pinball machine, and even a **car**.

Shaolin monk Feng Fei can throw a needle hard and fast enough to make a tiny hole in a pane of **glass**, creating shards that pop a **balloon** on the other side.

Built to look like London's Tower Bridge, the largest-ever LEGO sculpture contained more than **5.8 million individual pieces.**

Let's play!

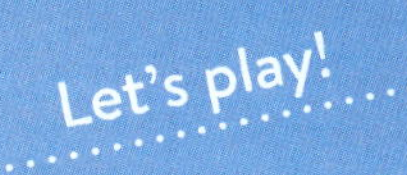

Stretching 102 miles (164km), the

WORLD'S LONGEST BRIDGE—

the Danyang-Kunshan Grand Bridge—connects the cities of Shanghai and Nanjing in China.

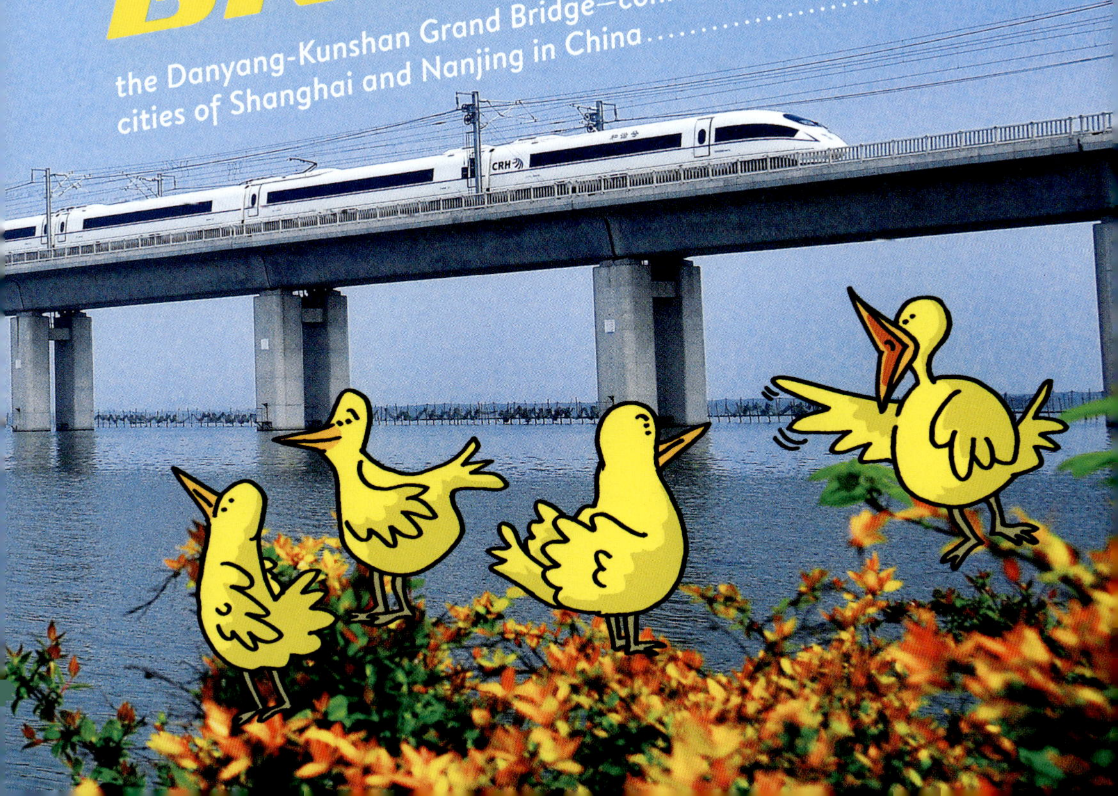

One competitor with

superspeedy fingers

solved a Rubik's Cube in just 3.13 seconds—the fastest time on record

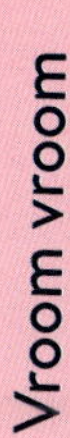

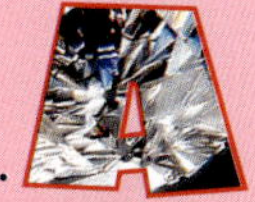

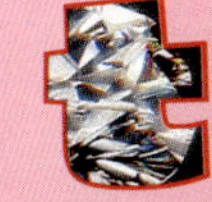

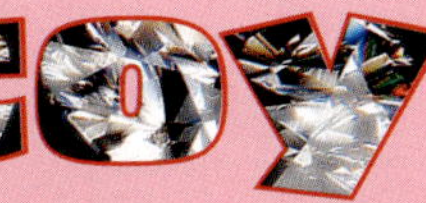

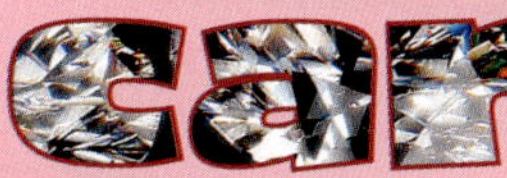

A toy car

made of white gold and encrusted in more than 2,700 diamonds sold for $60,000 at an auction.

Vroom vroom

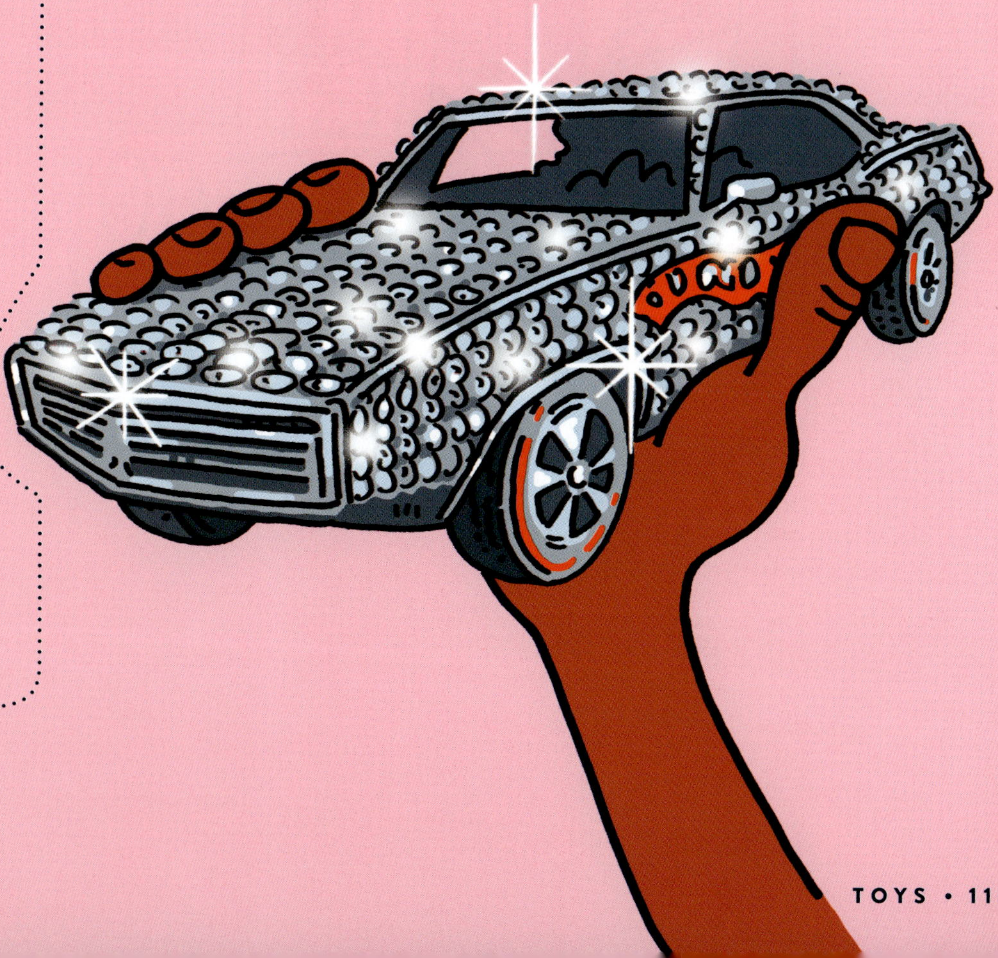

A 100-foot (30m) **superstretch limo**, equipped with 26 wheels and a mini golf course, is the world's longest car. It can fit 75 people inside . . .

Only one person could fit comfortably in the three-wheeled Peel P50, one of the **smallest cars ever built.**

A **monster-truck driver** made an epic jump over eight other monster trucks, in a vehicle called Megalodon . . .

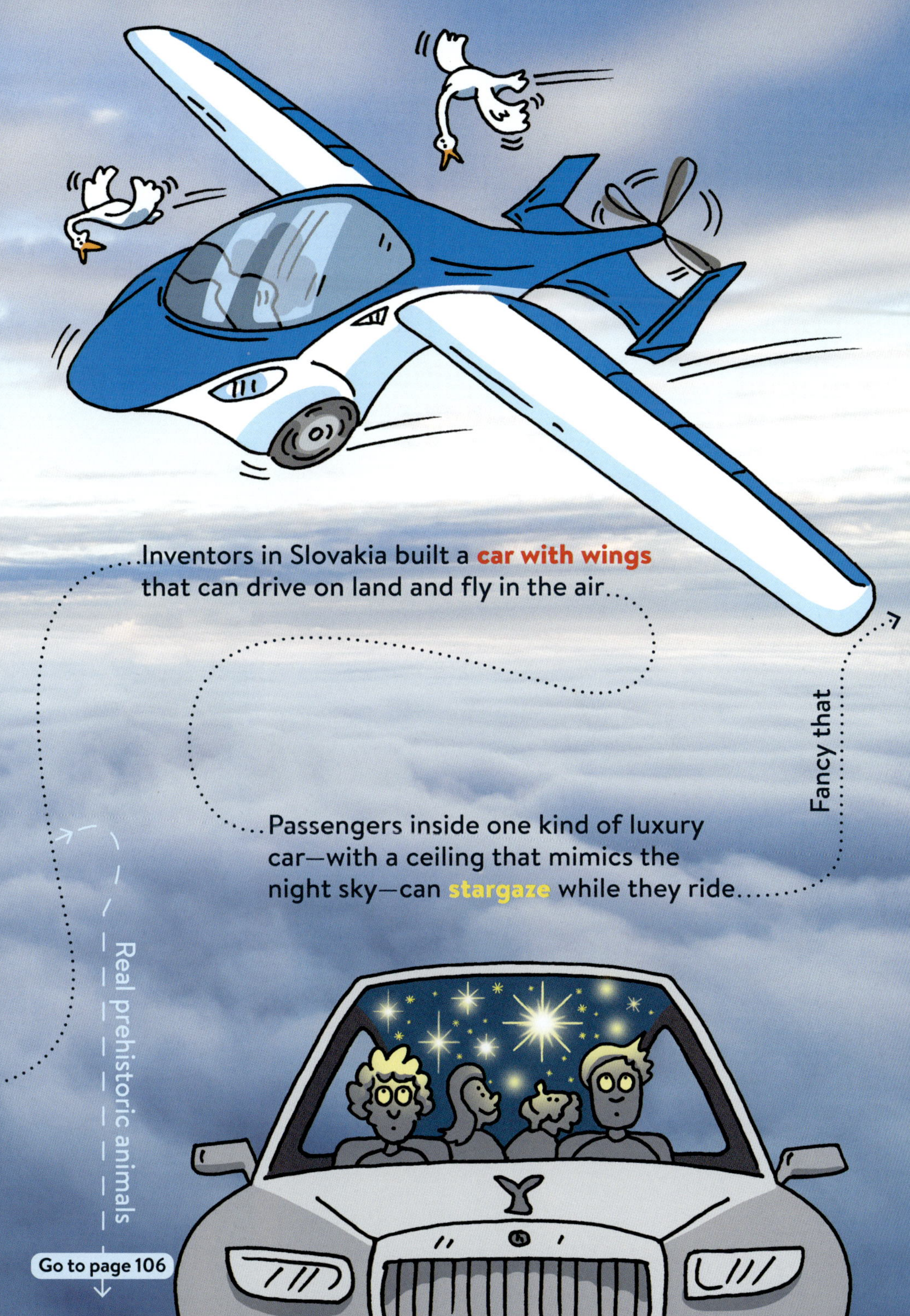

Inventors in Slovakia built a **car with wings** that can drive on land and fly in the air.

Passengers inside one kind of luxury car—with a ceiling that mimics the night sky—can **stargaze** while they ride.

Fancy that

Real prehistoric animals

Go to page 106

A concept for Aurora Station, the first **luxury space hotel,** included sleeping quarters for six people, who could see 16 sunrises a day from the hotel's windows.

A swimming pool shaped like a violin and fitted with more than **5,700 strands** of fiber-optic lights cost $1 million to build.

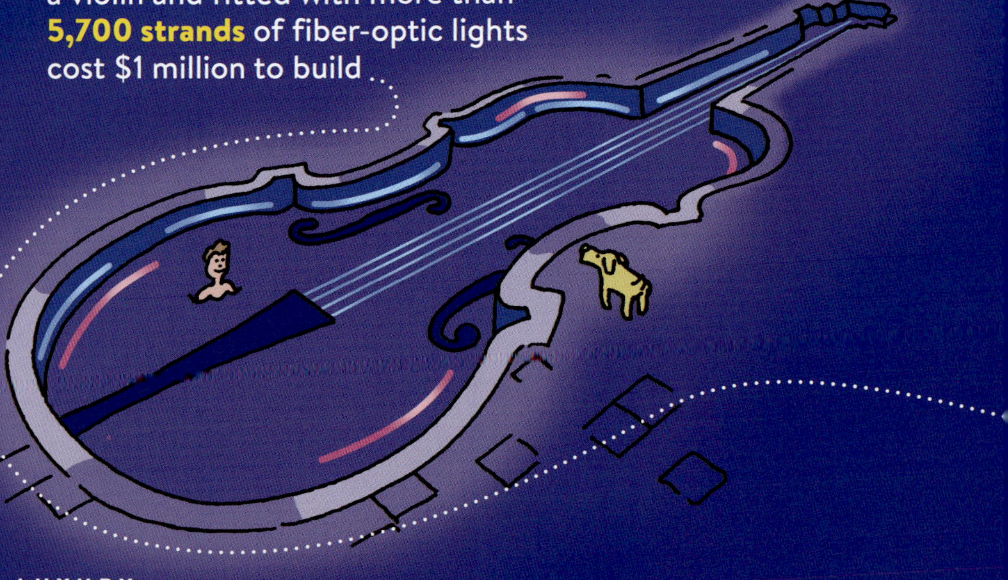

In Iceland, foodies can dine inside the
magma chamber
of a volcano.
Feeling hungry?

...A **giant weta bug** can scarf down an entire carrot in one meal...

...Hummingbirds are the world's hungriest birds—a human would have to eat the equivalent of **300 hamburgers** to match the bird's daily diet...

...Using only chopsticks, a contestant once ate **65 M&Ms in just one minute**...

...**Star-nosed moles** find and swallow food in the time it takes a person to blink—faster than any other mammal.......

...A type of bird called the bar-tailed godwit stores so much fat in its body before its annual migration that its **weight doubles**...

Time to go

Go to page 40

More extreme excursions

Wildebeests migrate across Africa's Serengeti each year, **dodging lions** as they search for

Traveling more than 20,000 miles (32,000km) roundtrip from **one end of Earth to the other**, each year the Arctic tern makes the longest known animal migration.

land to graze and fresh water to drink

Roar this way

A man in Sri Lanka once broke a stack of 12 **concrete** blocks using just his **head**.

Underneath a **bridge** in Seattle, Washington, is a giant troll crushing a real Volkswagen Beetle that has been encased in **concrete**.

Sculptures of two huge **hands** made of fiberglass and steel help to hold up a **bridge** in Vietnam.

A man in Bangladesh can balance a record-breaking 14 **tennis balls** on the back of his **hand**.

In China, there's an enormous sculpture of a lion carved out of a single **redwood tree**—an art piece that took 20 people three years to create.

In order to eat, a flamingo must position its **head upside down**.

Unlike humans, bats don't get dizzy from hanging **upside down** because their bodies don't weigh enough for gravity to affect the blood flowing to their heads.

Brilliant bodies

Some **salamanders** can regrow parts of their **brains** if they're damaged.

The **brains** of some of the largest dinosaurs ever to walk Earth—called titanosaurs—were only the size of a **tennis ball**.

Redwood trees are the tallest trees in the world and home to wandering **salamanders** that have adapted to parachute and glide through the air if they drop from their treetop perches.

Umbrella slugs, which live in the ocean, can have more than **700,000** teeth in their lifetime.

The ***longest human tongue*** stretches nearly 4 inches (10cm) outside the mouth.

Pit vipers have **special organs** between their noses and eyes that help them hunt at night by sensing heat from the bodies of their prey.

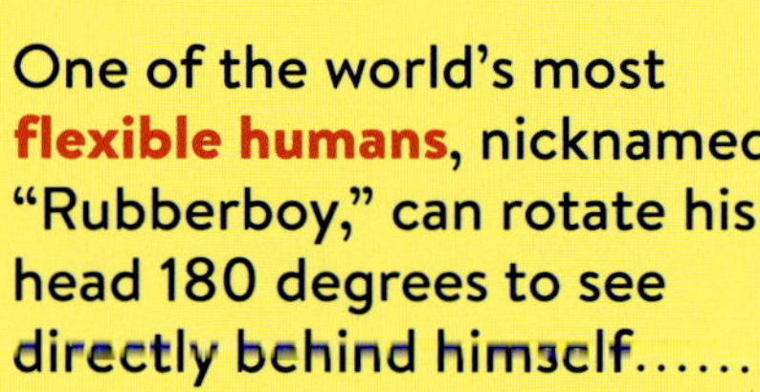

One of the world's most **flexible humans**, nicknamed "Rubberboy," can rotate his head 180 degrees to see directly behind himself.

Although it weighs just 1⅔ ounces (48g), the **hero shrew** has a backbone so strong it could hold the weight of a mountain goat.
Superstrong!

One of the world's strongest women holds a world record for using just her thighs to **crush three watermelons** in 7.5 seconds.

A hippopotamus can **pulverize a pumpkin** in its mouth with a single bite

An Australian man once held a **plank position** for 9½ hours—in this strength-testing position, only his toes and forearms were touching the ground!

A man from Pakistan once crushed **315 walnuts** in one minute using just his elbow...
One species of **tropical moss mite** can pull 530 times its own weight...
In the 19th century, one Canadian strongman pushed a train car uphill—he's still considered to be one of the **strongest humans** ever to live...
Get moving

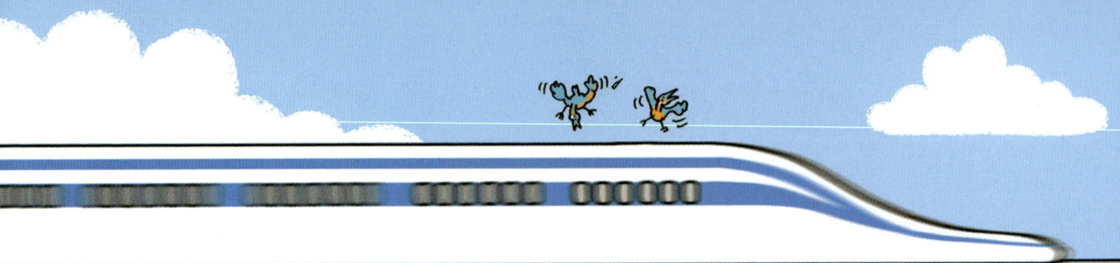

Japan's

LONG-NOSED BULLET TRAINS,

inspired by a kingfisher's pointed beak, can reach a speed of 375 miles an hour (604km/h).

Nicknamed "Mt. Goldsworthy," **the longest-ever train**—stretching 4½ miles (7.2km)—carried iron ore through Australia.

The Duge Bridge, which connects the provinces of Guizhou and Yunnan in China, holds the record for the **highest bridge in the world**, carrying travelers a staggering 1,800 feet (565 m) above the Beipan River below.

Go sky-high

The world's tallest skyscraper—the 2,717-foot (828m) Burj Khalifa in the United Arab Emirates—is also home to the world's **highest restaurant**, which serves oysters and caviar from 122 stories up.

Two skyscrapers in Hong Kong are nicknamed the "**koala buildings**"—the buildings' design makes each one look like several koalas hugging a tree.

A high-rise apartment building in Miami, Florida, has elevators not only for residents, but also for their cars. Apartment dwellers can **drive into an elevator** that will take their cars straight up to their home.

The U.S. Bank Tower in Los Angeles, California, once had a **glass slide** that people could ride down from the 70th to 69th floor.

Go to page 78

A tightrope walker once inched his way over **Niagara Falls** on live television.
An Austrian skydiver once made a parachute **jump from space** ...

In 1999, a daredevil on a motorcycle launched himself over the Grand Canyon, clearing the canyon and landing on the other side . . .
Do you dare?

A man once swam more than 3,000 miles (4,828km) through the
PIRANHA-INFESTED WATERS
of the Amazon River to set a world record for distance swimming.

A rock climber once scaled the sheer, vertical surface of El Capitan, a 3,000-foot (914m) cliff in California's Yosemite National Park, without ropes or a harness. He performed the **death-defying climb** in under four hours

Scale new heights

Every year, climbing guides on Mount Everest bring back about 28,000 pounds (12,700kg) of human poop—that's the weight of two male African elephants.

Vultures poop and pee on their own legs. The concoction is sterile and acts like hand sanitizer, getting rid of germs picked up from a messy meal of dead and rotting animal carcasses.

The legs of a centipede can regrow if the animal loses them. And some species grow more legs as they get older!

A duct tape festival takes place every year in Avon, Ohio, and features rides, a parade, and even a fashion show with clothes made entirely out of duct tape.

In one annual Australian fashion show, professional dressmakers doll up ducks in costumes inspired by fashion from the 1800s to today.

Laughter yoga is a type of exercise that's used to relieve stress.

Ducks from different places quack in different "accents"—quacks in one region may sound like giggling, while quacks in another region sound like shouting and laughter at the same time.

The world's largest centipede can climb up cave walls, hang from the ceiling, and catch and eat bats that fly by.

In a Utah cave, scientists found a 1,000-year-old piece of popcorn.

Popcorn was initially banned in American movie theaters until sound was introduced to cinema in the 1920s, which helped to drown out the crunching.

The Sol Cinema is a traveling movie theater that is entirely solar powered.

In 2016, the Solar Impulse 2 became the first solar-powered plane to fly approximately 25,000 miles (40,000km) around the world, fueled only by the sun.

Parts of a plane can be fixed with a special kind of tape that is built to withstand winds up to 600 miles an hour (966km/h).

One astronaut's yoga practice involved using bands and poles so she could stay in place while exercising in space.

Taking inspiration from a device used to train astronauts headed to space, one company proposed a design for a roller coaster that would have spots where riders would experience zero-gravity for up to eight seconds.

Wheeeeee!

On the Tower of Terror, located on the Gold Coast, Australia, riders drop at speeds of 100 miles an hour (161km/h) from nearly **38 stories high**

In Dallas, Texas, one ride dropped people one by one, **without a harness**, from 130 feet (40m) high on to a giant net

A waterslide in the Bahamas sends riders down a clear tube on a replica of an ancient temple and through a
SHARK-FILLED LAGOON
Surf's up

A Portuguese surfer once **rode a wave** that was taller than a ten-story building—the tallest wave ever surfed

In Pismo Beach, California, a goat named Pismo has learned to **balance on a surfboard**, once even catching a 9-foot (2.7m) wave.

Sense that?

The African elephant, which has a **brilliant sense of smell**, can detect water from over 12 miles (20km) away.

In cities such as London, U.K., some sidewalks can **generate power** by sensing and capturing energy from the impact of people's feet while they walk

Cool communities

Sea urchins have **no eyes**, but we know they can sense light because they respond to it by changing color or moving away

Try to survive

Go to page 86

To help the village's 24 residents feel less lonely, an artist in Nagoro, Japan, installed **350 human-size dolls** throughout the town

A building in Hamburg, Germany, is **powered using algae** that grow in panels down the side

In the city of Capri, Italy, it's illegal to leave dog poop on the ground—and city officials can use **DNA testing** to bust your pooch

It is illegal to hike naked in Switzerland.
It's illegal to lasso a fish in the stat

While there's no scientific proof that Bigfoot exists, a law in Washington State forbids anyone from killing the creature, should they see it.
of Tennessee.
Make a splash!

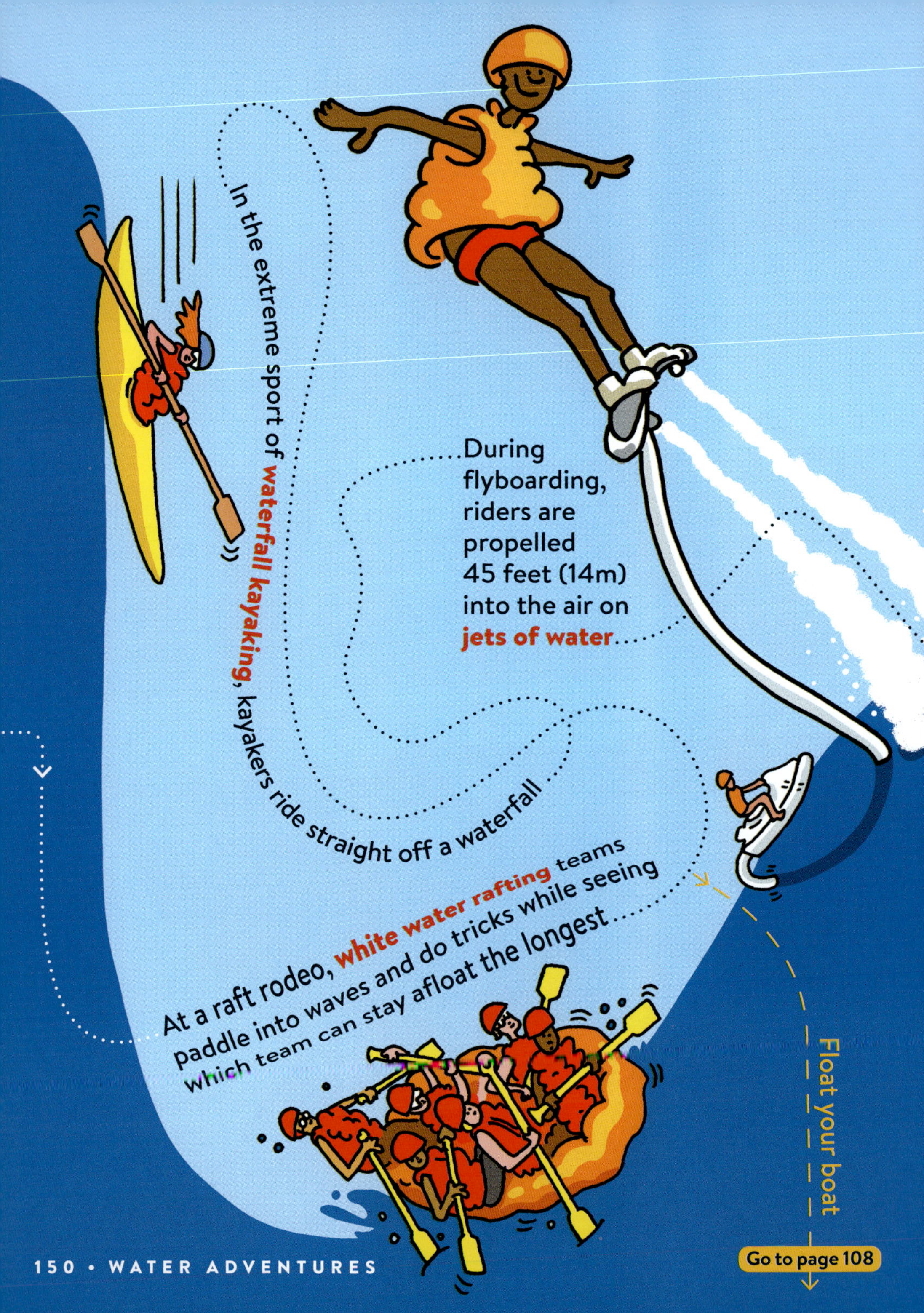

Go to page 108

In horse surfing, athletes riding a surfboard are pulled along the water by a galloping horse
In some tropical reefs, scuba divers can explore by underwater scooter.
Dive in

Hurricane Hunters are crews that fly specially designed **planes** directly into a hurricane. Scientists use the planes, which can measure temperature, air pressure, wind speed, and more, to learn about these destructive storms.

Every year, great white **sharks** migrate to a feeding spot in the Pacific Ocean that scientists have nicknamed "White Shark Café."

The cookiecutter **shark** latches its mouth on to its prey and spins it around in a circle, taking chunks shaped like **cookies** out of its flesh.

A golden **cookie** sign hanging over a German company's headquarters was stolen by someone dressed in a Cookie Monster costume. The sign was eventually found hanging around the neck of a local horse **statue**.

The Flying Pancake is a World-War-II-era **plane** that has a flat body—some think it could be the reason for alleged **UFO** sightings in the 1940s.

When a strange metal pillar appeared in a remote Utah desert, some thought it had been dropped there by a **UFO**!

So far away!

The U.S. government once tried to use a type of **silver** compound to control **hurricanes**.

Firefighting was once an event at the **Olympics**.

A three-headed dragon **statue** near a Russian theme park is nearly 50 feet (15m) tall and breathes real **fire**.

In the late 1800s, two brothers moved to **Inaccessible Island**—an extremely remote island in the South Atlantic Ocean—to hunt seals, but went home after many misadventures, including being pecked at and knocked over by the island's penguins!

To view the shipwrecked relics at the Pitcairn Island Museum, visitors

The Strombolicchio Lighthouse sits atop a former

VOLCANO

on a remote island in the Tyrrhenian Sea.....

Put on a display

must first take a **30-hour boat ride** through the South Pacific Ocean......

Go to page 12
This way up!
Built to celebrate **mountaineering**, the Messner Mountain Museum sits atop a cliff in northern Italy

At an underwater sculpture park off the coast of Grenada, a country in the Caribbean Sea, wetsuit-wearing visitors must breathe through air tanks to view the art.
Getting artsy

THE WORLD'S LARGEST STATUE—THE STATUE OF UNITY, IN INDIA—IS TALLER THAN 36 GIRAFFES STANDING ON TOP OF EACH OTHER

Artist Ai Weiwei created an artwork made up of **100 million tiny pieces of porcelain**, each individually painted to look like a sunflower seed

Japanese artist Azuma Makoto once sent a **bonsai tree** into space and kept it suspended using a helium balloon.

Tree-rific

In bloom

Go to page 82

The Chapel Oak, an ancient tree in France, gets its name from **two small churches** nestled inside its trunk.

Pando, a massive colony of aspen-tree clones with roots spreading across more than 100 acres (40ha), is one of the world's largest living organisms—all 40,000 tree clones originated from a **single seed**.

Old man's beard is a type of lichen, a plantlike organism, that hangs from tree branches and can grow up to 20 feet (6m) long.
That looks fluffy

Chinchillas, rodents with the world's softest fur, have up to 75 hairs in each follicle. They roll around in dust baths to remove dirt and oils from their coat.

Some dog groomers take petcare to a new level, spending days to

PRIMP A POOCH

into looking like a flamingo or a clown

Fancy some pampering?

After making appearances in music videos and advertisements, one of **Taylor Swift's cats**, called Olivia Benson, is worth roughly $97 million.

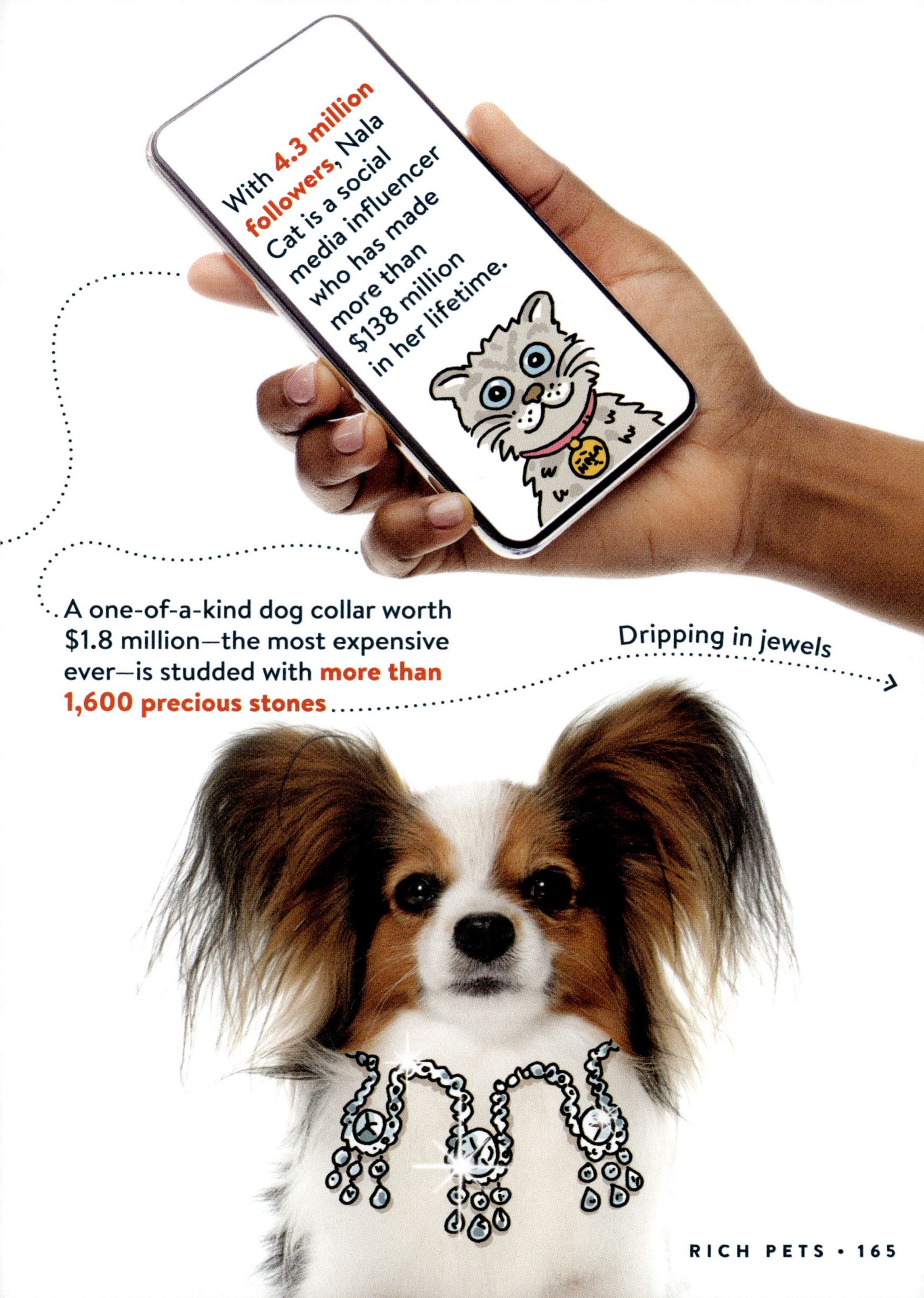
With **4.3 million followers**, Nala Cat is a social media influencer who has made more than $138 million in her lifetime.
A one-of-a-kind dog collar worth $1.8 million—the most expensive ever—is studded with **more than 1,600 precious stones**
Dripping in jewels

The **largest diamond** ever found, called the Cullinan, weighs more than a soccer ball...

A skeleton found inside a lavish Mesopotamian tomb belonging to a queen was draped in **gold and precious stones**—together, everything she wore weighed more than a Yorkshire terrier...

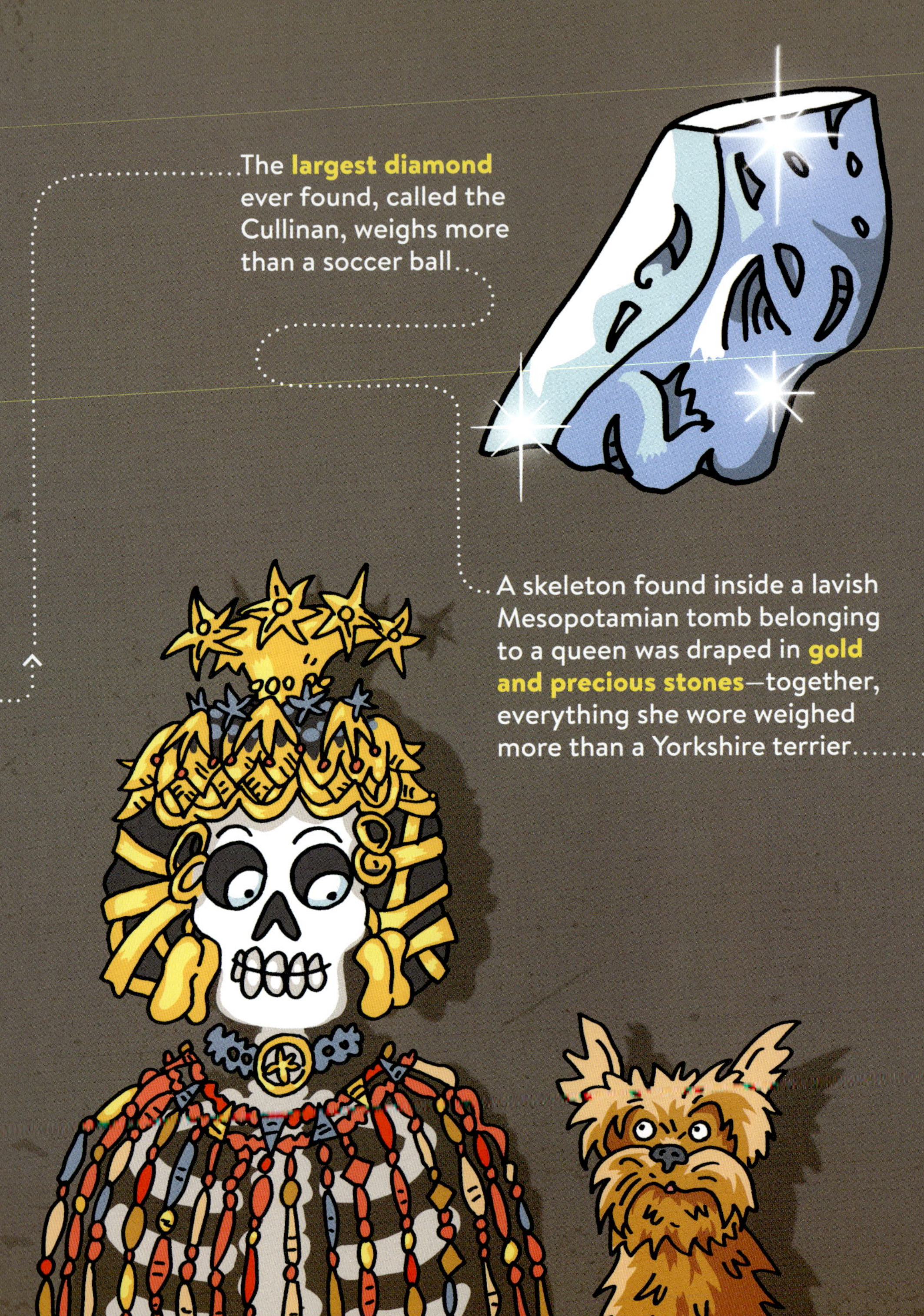

Many mummies in ancient Egypt were buried with **emeralds around their necks** because legend had it that the stones were said to bring rebirth and protection . . .

Such a legend

A legend in Mesopotamia said that the Big Weather Beast, a **lion-headed demon** with bird feet and fangs, could control the weather and keep cities free from diseases.

To help buildings sustain extreme weather events, researchers developed bendable **glass** that's 200 times stronger than regular glass.

A **glass** bridge holding a giant **diamond**-shaped restaurant dangles over a canyon in the country of Georgia.

Some people in ancient China used **diamonds** to polish ceremonial stone **axes**.

Dinosaur fossils have been to **space**.

Scientists in **space** are able to measure the glow of holiday **lights** down on Earth because they are so bright.

There's a **light** bulb in a California fire station that's been shining for more than 120 years. It's always on to make sure there's light on the **fire trucks**.

One 1940s **fire truck** has been outfitted with jet **engines**—it can reach speeds of up to 407 miles an hour (655km/h).

The smallest working steam **engine** was made in a lab by scientists—it's one-tenth the width of a strand of human **hair**.

The world's largest ball of **hair** was removed from the stomach of a **cow**. The record-breaking hair ball weighed 55 pounds (25kg).

The world's largest **axe**, in New Brunswick, Canada, is made of 55 tons (50t) of **steel** and is stuck in a giant stump that's used to stage concerts and plays.

The four deadly **spikes** on the tails of **dinosaurs** like the *Stegosaurus* are called a thagomizer.

A man nicknamed "Crusher" set a record for bending 14 **steel spikes** in just one minute.

There is a herd of wild **cows** that lives on the grounds of a **castle** in England. The herd's ancestors have lived there since medieval times.

Many people in **Panama** consider the poisonous golden frog a symbol of good luck.

Feeling lucky?

One man built a **castle** out of thousands of plastic bottles in **Panama**. It has four bedrooms, a dining room, and even a dungeon.

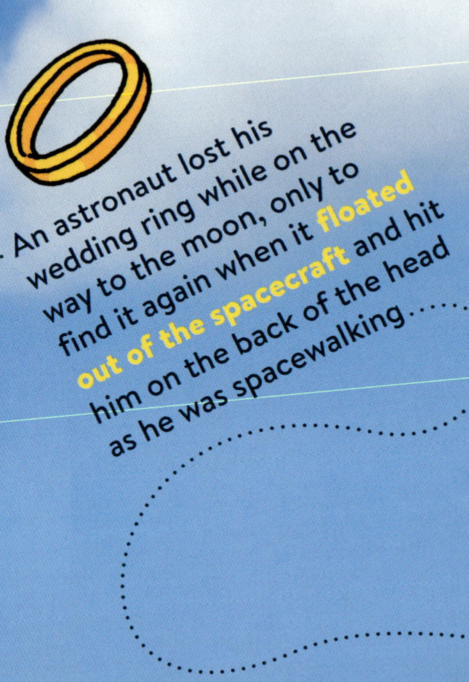

An astronaut lost his wedding ring while on the way to the moon, only to find it again when it **floated out of the spacecraft** and hit him on the back of the head as he was spacewalking

A British scientist **discovered penicillin**, a medicine used to treat infections, in part by a lucky accident—he returned from holiday to find that a mold that had grown in his lab was killing bacteria

Though the odds of finding a lucky **four-leaf clover** are around 1 in 10,000, one lady found 21 in her front yard in a single day

Rad reflections
Ancient Romans believed that gods saw humans' souls through mirrors, which is the origin of the superstition that breaking a mirror is bad luck.
In some parts of Europe, pigs made of candy are often gifted to wish people luck for the New Year.

Legend has it that the
ancient Greeks
used large mirrors as **heat rays** to focus the

A mysterious jet airplane

with a mirrorlike covering has been spotted flying over the Mojave Desert in the southwestern part of the U.S.A.

The first people to cross the English Channel in a **hot-air balloon** brought so much stuff that the balloon stayed low and almost crashed. In panic, the passengers threw almost everything overboard—including their jackets and pants

Relative to its size, an Anna's hummingbird can fly

FASTER THAN A FIGHTER JET!

The bird can travel 385 times its body length in a single second.

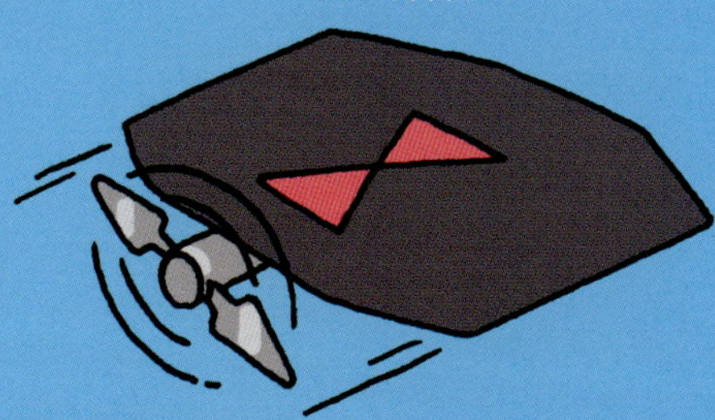

The world's **smallest spy plane**, outfitted with a tiny video camera, could fit in the palm of your hand.

More daring defenses

Balloon party!

Go to page 184

Giant armadillos fight off enemies and tear through termite mounds with an 8-inch (20cm) **hooked claw** on each front foot, the longest of any animal.

Pygmy sperm whales create a **cloud of poop** to confuse predators while they make a quick exit.

Back in the old days

To reach Kalavantin Durg—an ancient fortress near Mumbai, India—attackers would have had to make a dangerous trek that involves scrambling up steep inclines and scaling **zigzagging stairs**...

Uluru, an ancient sandstone rock in Australia, appears to **CHANGE COLORS** throughout the day, from red to orange to purple.

Petra, an ancient city in Jordan, contains **tombs and temples** that were carved painstakingly into the sides of pink sandstone cliffs.

Look at that!

Assorted **horse toys** mysteriously appeared in a circle formation at a site in Lincoln, Massachusetts, earning it the nickname "Ponyhenge"

Belgium's highways are some of the **most illuminated** in the world—they have 150,000 lampposts with 335,000 lights. These roads are so bright that they can even be seen from space.

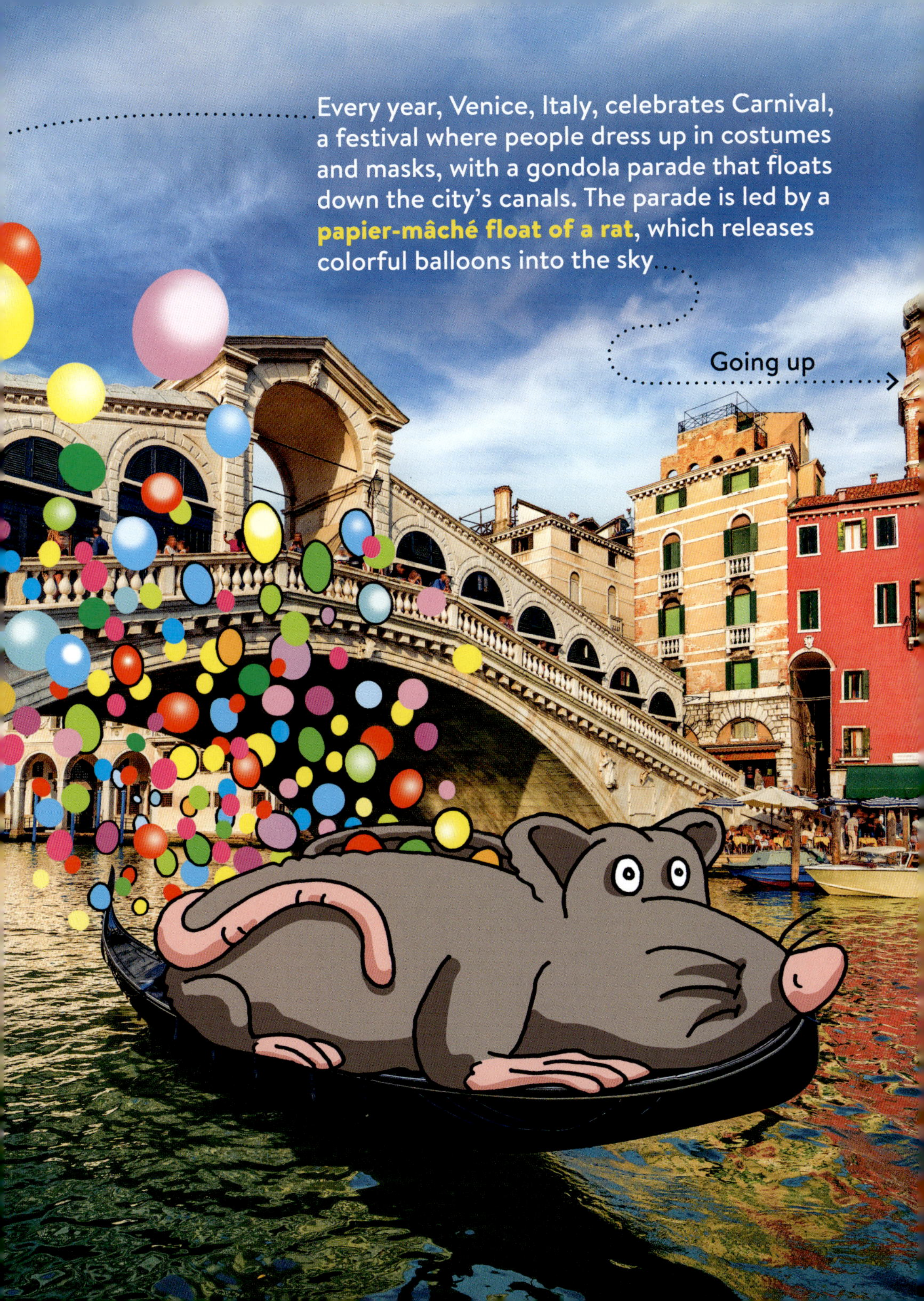

Every year, Venice, Italy, celebrates Carnival, a festival where people dress up in costumes and masks, with a gondola parade that floats down the city's canals. The parade is led by a **papier-mâché float of a rat**, which releases colorful balloons into the sky...

Going up

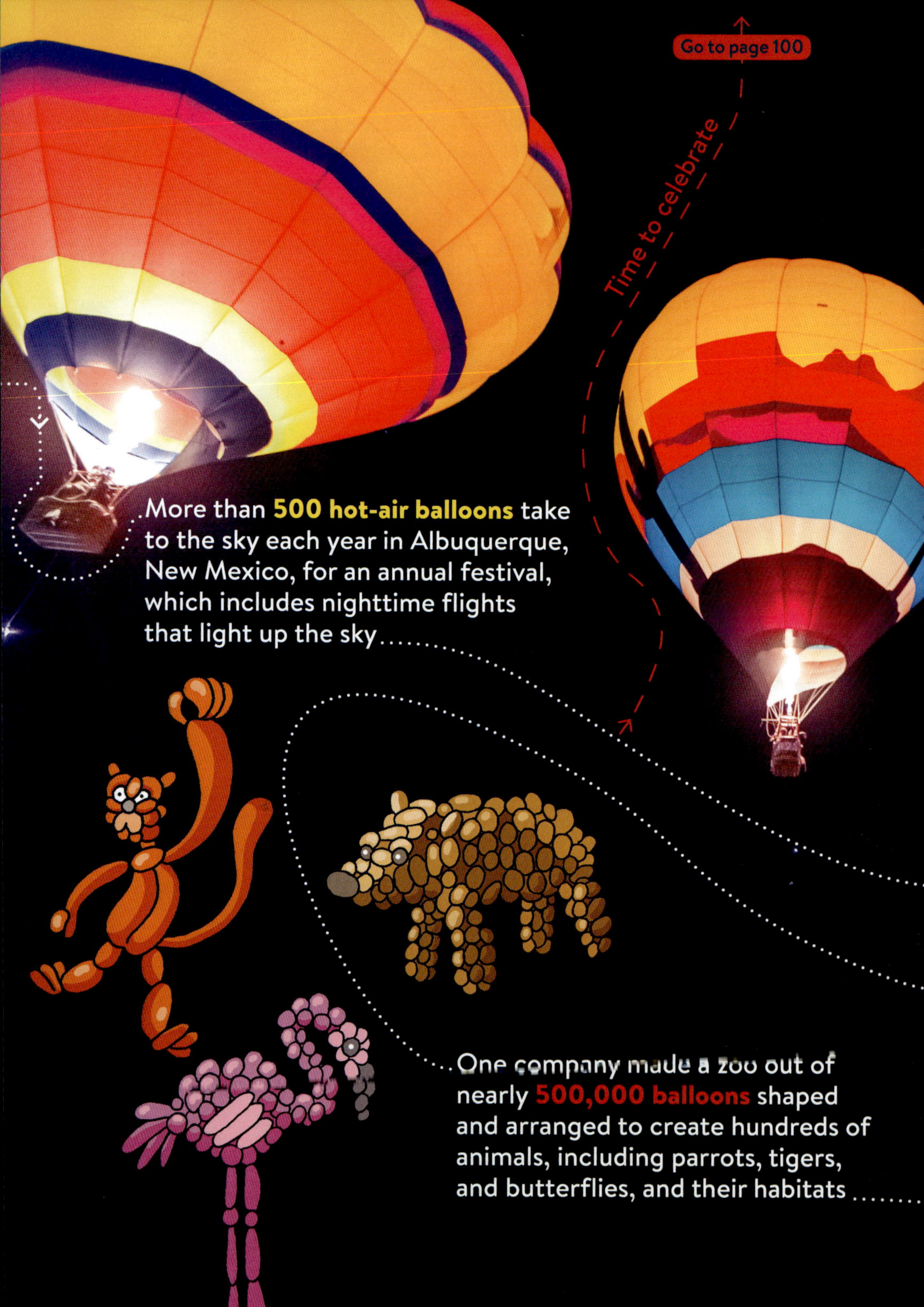

Time to celebrate
Go to page 100

More than **500 hot-air balloons** take to the sky each year in Albuquerque, New Mexico, for an annual festival, which includes nighttime flights that light up the sky

One company made a zoo out of nearly **500,000 balloons** shaped and arranged to create hundreds of animals, including parrots, tigers, and butterflies, and their habitats

As an elaborate April Fools' Day prank, a UFO-shaped hot-air balloon was flown over London, prompting many people to report sightings of **extraterrestrial activity**

To the zoo

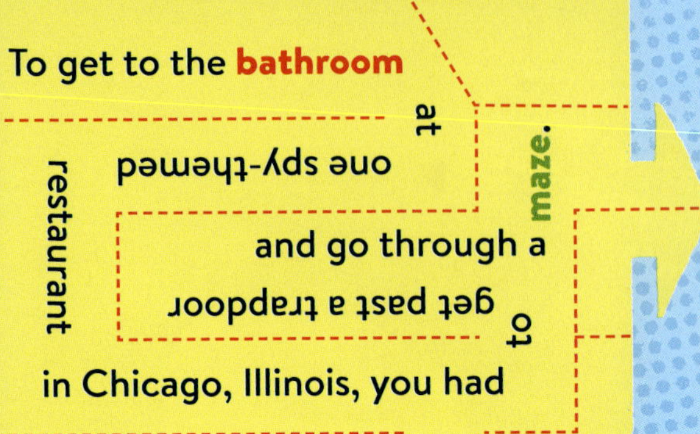

The Pineapple Garden **Maze** in Oahu, Hawaii, features 14,000 native Hawaiian plants plus vegetation arranged to look like a **pineapple** in the center.

During a hurricane, the Miami Zoo in Florida kept their flamingos safe by putting them in a **bathroom**.

In a park in Moscow, Russia, couples have put thousands of **padlocks**, resembling "leaves," onto iron **tree** frames as a symbol of their love.

Kapok **trees** are the largest in the **rainforest** and can add up to 13 feet (4m) to their height each year—more than twice the size of an average adult human.

A giant **pineapple**-shaped building in South Africa is the world's largest pineapple building and features a **museum** honoring the tangy fruit.

Leeds Castle in England features a **museum** devoted entirely to **dog collars**.

Dog collars in 18th-century North America sometimes had **padlocks** on them for which only the owner had the key.

In Costa Rica's **rainforest**, visitors can stay at a tree-house hotel that was built from the body of a real **airplane** and is surrounded by toucans, monkeys, and other wildlife.

In 1964, a B-52 **airplane** lost its entire tail due to extreme turbulence over New Mexico, but it still managed to land safely six hours later.

Other amazing tails

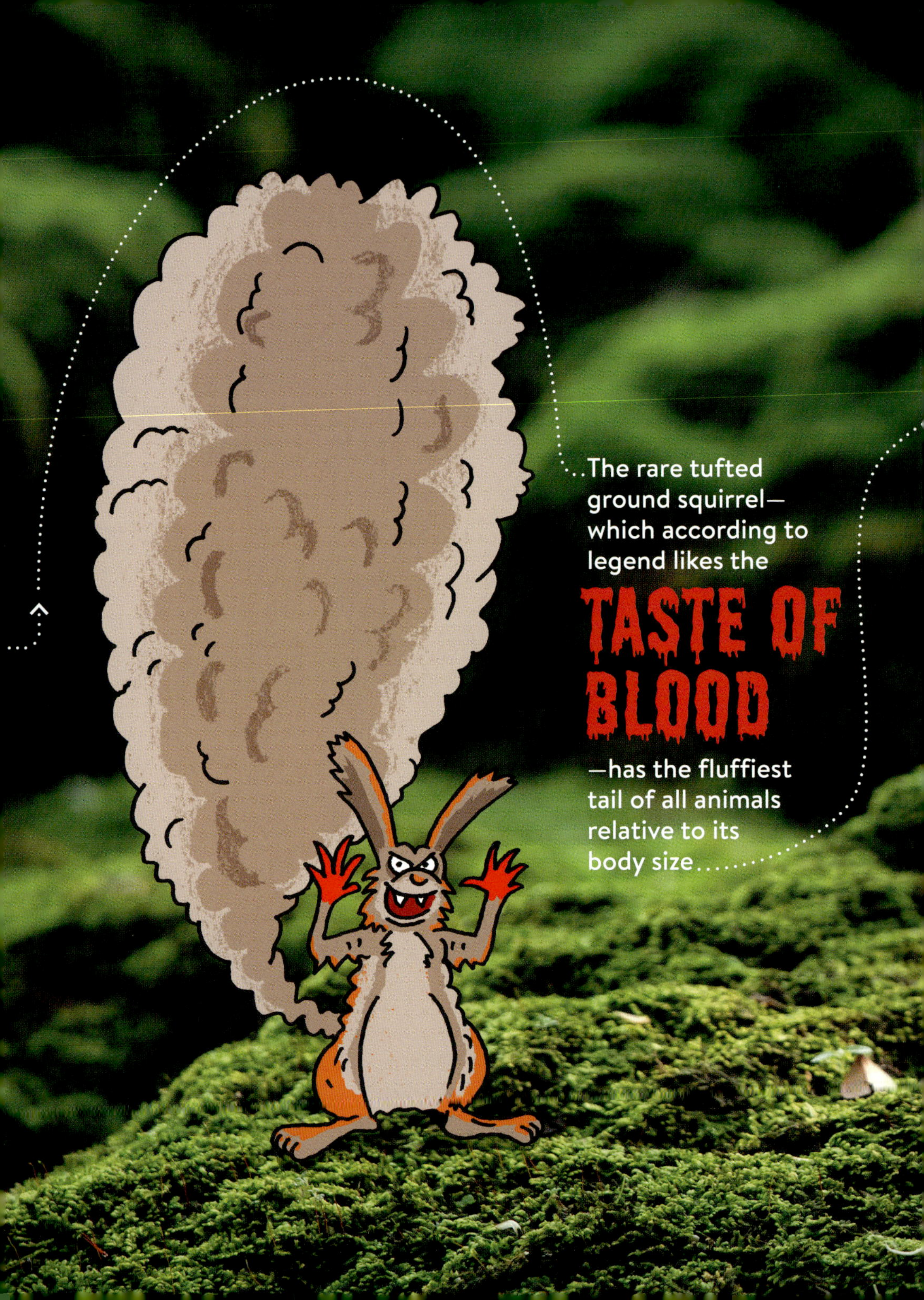
The rare tufted ground squirrel—which according to legend likes the
TASTE OF BLOOD
—has the fluffiest tail of all animals relative to its body size . . . . . .

AN ARMORED DINOSAUR

called a Stegouros, found in southern Chile, had a bladed tail

Get some protection

An artist in Calgary, Canada, creates armor for

Cats and Mice

More masterpieces
Go to page 158

Pangolins, covered from head to tail with hundreds of **tough scales**, roll up in a protective ball when threatened

Bugging out

A fungus-eating desert insect called the **diabolical ironclad beetle** has wings but doesn't fly—instead, the wings are permanently fused together and act as protective armor...

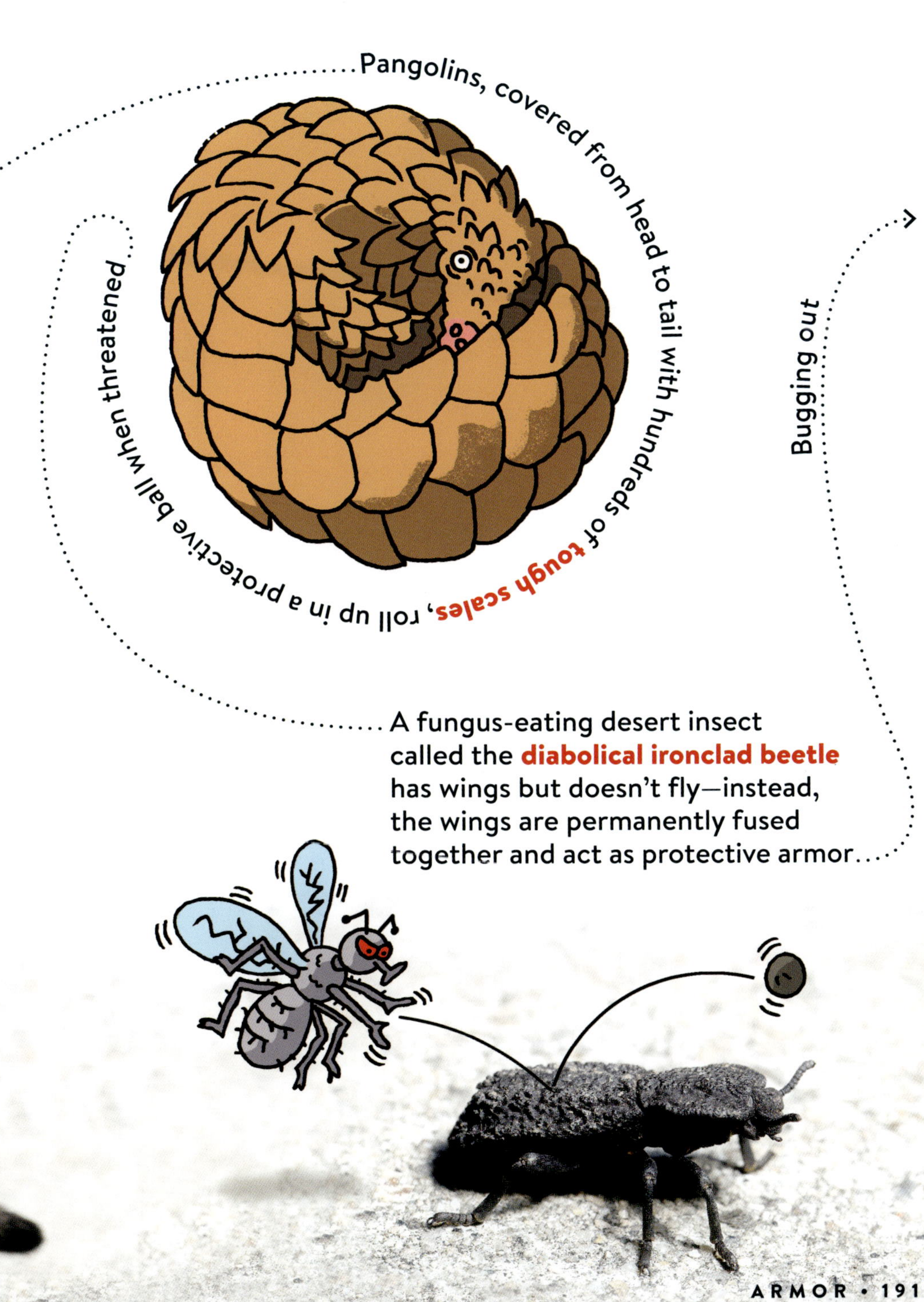

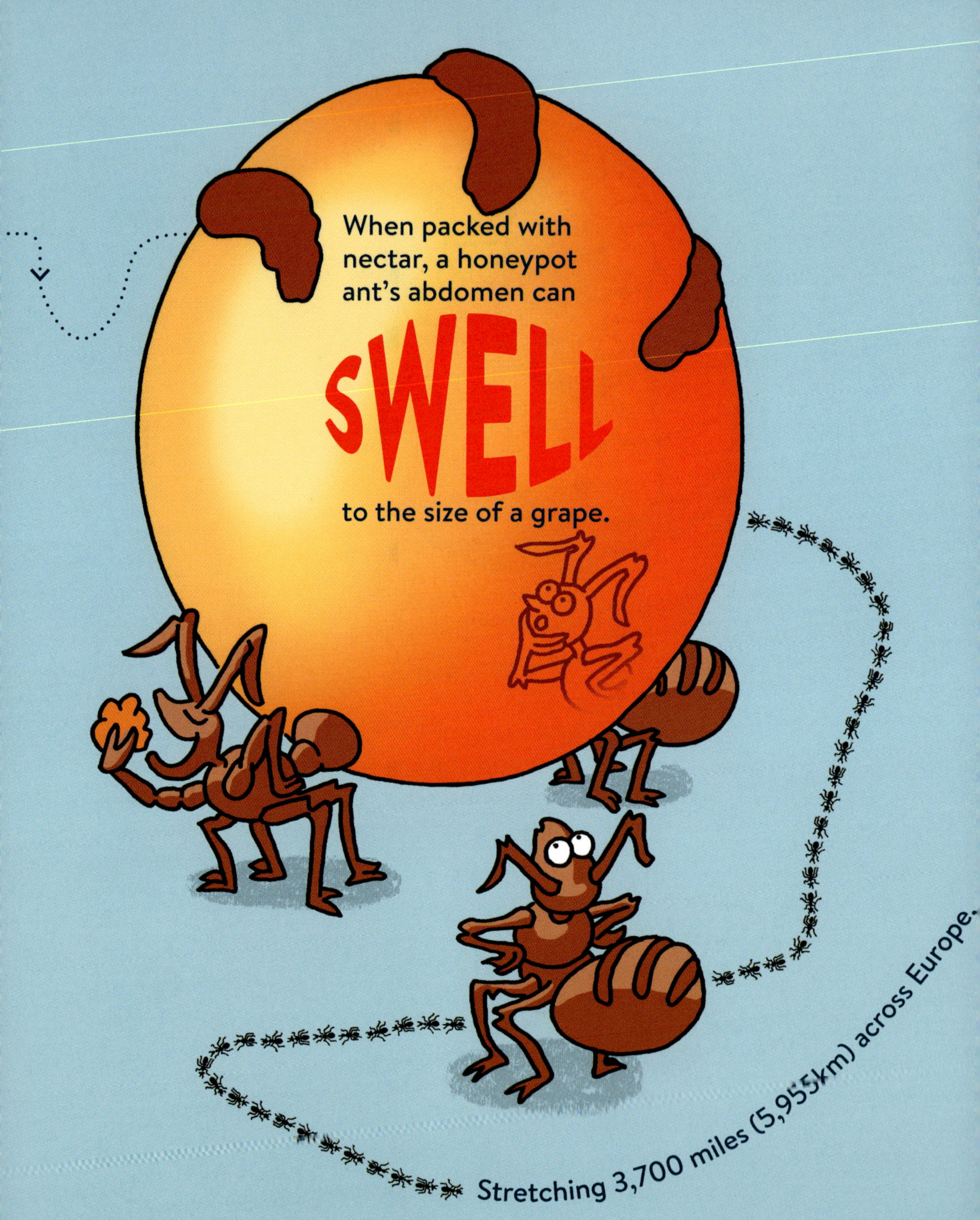
When packed with nectar, a honeypot ant's abdomen can
SWELL
to the size of a grape.
Stretching 3,700 miles (5,955km) across Europe.

…group of millions of Argentine ants formed the **largest-ever colony**…

RoboBees—tiny robots weighing about as much as a honeybee—are small enough to fit on a human fingernail…

That's hi-tech

Go to page 64

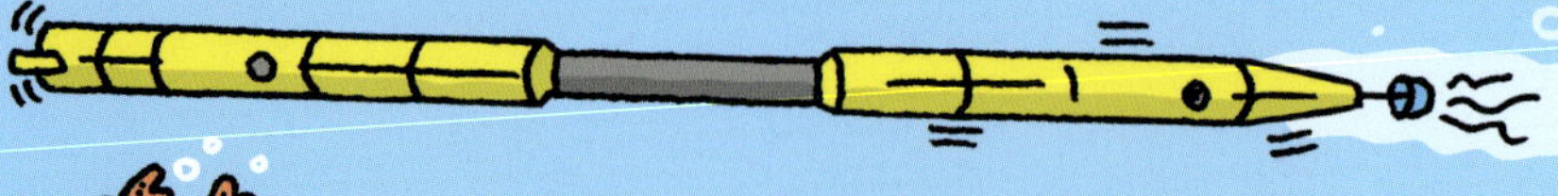

A robot shaped like a **giant pencil** was deployed in Antarctica to monitor melting glaciers

Brr!

Sophia, a humanoid robot that uses **artificial intelligence** to draw people's portraits, was declared a citizen of Saudi Arabia

Use and reuse!

Researchers at a university created a robot that can **help with recycling**—it can detect whether an object is paper, metal, or plastic just by holding it . . .

One of the world's softest robots—which resembles an **eight-legged sea creature with tentacles** and is called "octobot"—was partially built using a 3D printer . . .

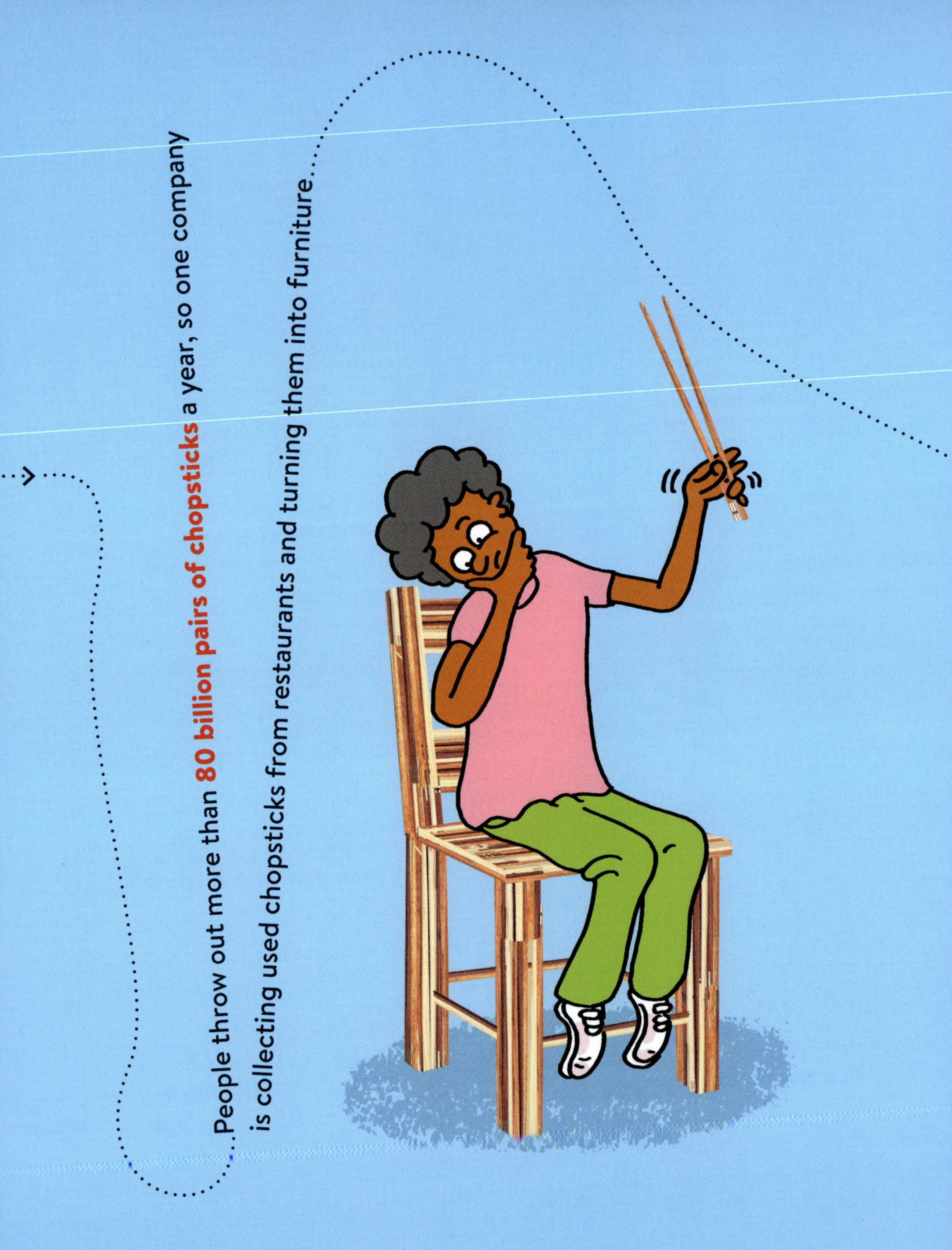

People throw out more than **80 billion pairs of chopsticks** a year, so one company is collecting used chopsticks from restaurants and turning them into furniture.

What goes up

Architects want to **build a skyscraper** in London, U.K., that would use plastic, glass, and paper recycled by its residents as building materials to eventually fill in the walls of higher floors.

Starting from 76 stories above ground, the **highest bungee jump** plummets people straight from the top of Macau Tower in China. Jumpers experience free fall for about 6 seconds!

Index

Meet the FACTopians

Rose Davidson is a writer and editor based in Cincinnati, Ohio. The author of multiple children's books, she loves writing stories about wild-animal behaviors and the mind-boggling beauty of our natural world. While writing this book, she enjoyed researching a wide range of subjects, including some of her personal favorites: wildlife, space, history, technology, and food. Rose's sweet tooth was thrilled to learn that the biggest ice-cream cone was taller than a basketball hoop. Yum!

Andy Smith is an award-winning illustrator. A graduate of the Royal College of Art, London, U.K., he creates artwork that has an optimistic, handmade feel. Creating the illustrations for *Epic FACTopia!* has brought even more surprises, from guitar-shaped boats to skydivers from space! Andy loves tomatoes, so his favorite fact to draw was La Tomatina, the world's biggest food fight.

Lawrence Morton is an art director and graphic designer based in rural Suffolk, U.K. He loves designing and has worked on all sorts of projects, from posters for punk bands to fashion magazines and cook books. He was excited by tales of climbing in California's Yosemite National Park but alarmed at tales of swimming in piranha-infested waters. He has always loved a spectacular firework show and enjoyed the fact about the enormous fireworks at Japan's Katakai Festival.

Sources

Scientists, historians, and other experts are discovering new facts and updating information all the time. That's why our *FACTopia* team has checked that every fact that appears in this book is based on multiple trustworthy sources and has been verified by a team of Britannica fact checkers. Of the hundreds of sources used in this book, here is a list of key websites we consulted.

News Organizations

apnews.com
bbc.com
bbcearth.com
businessinsider.com
cnn.com
cntraveler.com
dailymail.co.uk
discovermagazine.com
earthsky.org
livescience.com
nationalgeographic.com
nationalgeographic.org
newscientist.com
npr.org
nytimes.com
pbs.org
sciencealert.com
sciencedaily.com
sciencedirect.com
sciencefocus.com
sciencenews.org
theguardian.com
usatoday.com
washingtonpost.com
vox.com
wired.com

Government, Scientific, and Academic Organizations

britannica.com
eurekalert.org
fs.usda.gov
journals.aps.org
jpl.nasa.gov
kids.britannica.com
leakeyfoundation.org
nasa.gov
noaa.gov
nature.org
pnas.org
usgs.gov
nps.gov

Museums and Zoos

animals.sandiegozoo.org
montereybayaquarium.org
nhm.ac.uk
si.edu
smithsonianmag.com
whitbymuseum.org.uk

Universities

hort.extension.wisc.edu
ipm.missouri.edu
ucmp.berkeley.edu
ufl.edu

Other Websites

cbc.ca
cnet.com
discoverwildlife.com
guinnessworldrecords.com
ripleys.com
atlasobscura.com
lonelyplanet.com
mentalfloss.com
modernfarmer.com
newatlas.com
redbull.com
scienceabc.com
sciencefriday.com
space.com
theconversation.com
thespruce.com

Picture Credits

The publisher would like to thank the following for permission to reproduce their photographs and illustrations. While every effort has been made to credit images, the publisher apologizes for any errors or omissions and will be pleased to make any necessary corrections in future editions of the book.

t = top; c = center; b = bottom

Back cover: Canaplus_M.Faba/iStockphoto

p.3 Marat Musabirov/iStockphoto; p.6 Zhenikeyev/iStockphoto; p.9 Marti Bug Catcher/Shutterstock; pp.10–11 Nastco/iStockphoto; pp.12–13 Cavan Images/Alamy; p.14 Cultura Creative Ltd/Alamy; pp.16–17 Arina P Habich/Shutterstock; p.19 parameter/iStockphoto; p.20 NASA; p.21 Leamus/iStockphoto; p.22 Nadia Uyoung/Shutterstock; p.23 Eric Mischke/iStockphoto; p.24 SeanXu//iStockphoto; p.25 NASA/GRC/Christopher Lynch; p.26 dagsjo/iStockphoto; p.28 dottedhippo/iStockphoto; p.29 zorazhung/iStockphoto; p.30 xenotar/iStockphoto; p.32 (silk) AlexeyVs/iStockphoto; p.32 (stones) Azure-Dragon/iStockphoto; p.34 robynmac/iStockphoto; p.36 incrediVFX/iStockphoto; p.37 Jun/iStockphoto; p.39t motimeiri/iStockphoto; p.39c&b Parinya_romeo61/iStockphoto; p.40 Thomas Worsley/Alamy; p.41 Jatuphot Phuatawee/Alamy; p.44 Pelikh Alexey/Shutterstock; p.45 Canaplus_M.Faba/iStockphoto; p.46 Zhenikeyev/iStockphoto; p.49 Pavliha/iStockphoto; p.50 undefined undefined/iStockphoto; p.52 BIOSPHOTO/Alamy; pp.54–55 mammuth/iStockphoto; p.57 GregD/Shutterstock; p.58 efks/iStockphoto; p.59 maudanros/Shutterstock; pp.60–61 Wirestock Creators/Shutterstock; p.62 JaviJ/iStockphoto; p.64 Alex Kova/Alamy; p.65 FlashMovie/iStockphoto; p.66 SciePro/Shutterstock; p.67 Nerthuz/iStockphoto; p.71 Rudmer Zwerver/Shutterstock; pp.72–73 Athena345T/iStockphoto; pp.74–75 sololos/iStockphoto; p.75 NASA; p.78 Sahara Frost/Shutterstock; p.79 321photography/iStockphoto; p.80 Westend61 GmbH/Alamy; p.85t HUNG CHIN LIU/iStockphoto; p.85b djgis/Shutterstock; pp.86–87 spooh/iStockphoto; p.88 scisettialfio/iStockphoto; p.89t Obatala photography/Shutterstock; p.89b Rajesh A/iStockphoto; p.90 kimberrywood/Shutterstock; p.92 unalozmen/iStockphoto; p.93 Lalocracio/iStockphoto; pp.94–95 Haovo Wang/Shutterstock; pp.96–97 Hemis/Alamy; p.99 Jennifer Watson/iStockphoto; p.100 Alfo Co.Ltd/Alamy; p.102c gaffera/iStockphoto; p.102b bembodesign/iStockphoto; p.103t julichka/iStockphoto; p.103b Asergieiev/iStockphoto; p.104 baona/iStockphoto; p.106 ULADZIMIR ZGURSKI/iStockphoto; p.108 Bim/iStockphoto; p.109 BrianSantlebury/iStockphoto; pp.112–113 Imaginechina Limited/Alamy; pp.116–117 bjdlzx/iStockphoto; pp.118 buradaki/iStockphoto; p.119 Alisa_Ch/Shutterstock; p.120 valentinarr/iStockphoto; pp.122–123 blinkwinkel/Alamy; p.124 Zrfphoto/Dreamstime; p.125 CraigRJD/iStockphoto; p.126 Jun Zhang/Shutterstock; p.127 deimagine/iStockphoto; p.128 GlobalP/iStockphoto; p.129tl Milen Gagov/iStockphoto; p.129tr Marat Musabirov/iStockphoto; p.130 Beyondimages/iStockphoto; p.131 holgs/iStockphoto; p.132 Denys.Kutsevalov/Shutterstock; p.134 cokada/iStockphoto; p.135 wsfurlan/iStockphoto; pp.136–137t SL_Photography/iStockphoto; pp.136–137b AegeanBlue/iStockphoto; p.137 omikscovsky/Shutterstock; p.138 jskiba/iStockphoto; pp.140–141 sbayram/iStockphoto; p.143 StevenDillon/iStockphoto; p.144 Marieke Peche/iStockphoto; p.146 imageBROKER.com GmbH & Co.KG/Alamy; pp.146–147 SymbiosisArtmedia/Shutterstock; p.149 bbevren/iStockphoto; p.152 Vikks/Shutterstock; pp.154–155 thomaslenne/iStockphoto; pp.156–157 MoLarjung/Shutterstock; p.157 R Gombarik/Shutterstock; p.158 robertharding/Alamy; p.159 studio023/iStockphoto; p.161 DaveWalker/Shutterstock; p.163 Natallia Yaumenenka/Shutterstock; p.164 Robert Daly/iStockphoto; p.165t Prostock-Studio/iStockphoto; p.165b cynoclub/iStockphoto; pp.168–169 natthanim/iStockphoto; p.171 Ernie James/Alamy; pp.172–173 Evgeniy Skripnichenko/iStockphoto; p.173 Micha Klootwijk/Dreamstime; pp.174–175 magann/iStockphoto; p.177 Thomas Morris/Shutterstock; p.179 Mohnish Maurya/Shutterstock; pp.180–181 vovashevchuk/iStockphoto; p.182 NicoElNino/iStockphoto; p.183 Andrew Mayovskyy/Shutterstock; pp.184–185 robertharding/Alamy; p.186 FedotovAnatoly/iStockphoto; p.187 Design Pics Inc/Alamy; p.188 Rattankun Thongbun/iStockphoto; p.190 GlobalP/iStockphoto; p.191 Heather Broccard-Bell/iStockphoto; p.193 Marina mrs_brooke/Shutterstock; p.194 Anton Gvozdikov/Shutterstock; p.195 Veronika Ryabova/iStockphoto; p.196 onairjiw/iStockphoto; p.197 (glass bottles) mbongorus iStockphoto; p.197 (plastic bottles) Picsfive/iStockphoto; p.197 (cardboard) Alexan2008/iStockphoto; pp.198–199 cozyta/Shutterstock.